MYTH- X

One Fan's Interpretation of the X-Files' Mytharc

Michelle Bush

ISBN 978-1-4357-4688-6

Dedicated to my husband Greg and the members
of the Myth-X email list.

...and yes, I do have a life.

NOTES & ACKNOWLEDGEMENTS

Those of you who have read *Myth-X* in one of its previous incarnations on either the website (www.myth-x.org) or the e-book during the run of the show will find that based on the final few episodes, some of my ideas have changed–or more accurately–solidified in a manner that is slightly different from my initial analysis. Do I still believe that the show's mytharc narrative is mythic? Yes, I do. Would I have rather Mulder and Scully had kept their son and realized their "truth?" Definitely, although a part of me reluctantly understands why Chris Carter chose the ending he did. Hopefully I will be able to explain that position in what follows. Do I believe that everyone should agree with me? Not even remotely. Myths and stories are personal things, each assimilated according to one's own beliefs and biases. What I do hope, is that by reading *Myth-X* one might be able to step back and watch the show through different eyes.

I know I've learned a great deal from all of the discussions and debates that I've engaged in over the years. This is dedicated to those folks who took the time to engage in those debates and who inspired me to take a fresh look at the story; and without whom I would have never seen the show as anything more than an entertaining, if somewhat baffling, hour out of my Sunday evening. Special thanks go to the patient members of the *Myth-X* email list, my husband Greg, and my wonderful friend Annelies, all of whom were subjected to both my ranting and my theories as they formed, many times out of incoherent ramblings. No one challenged me more than they did and for that I am very grateful. And finally my gratitude to Exobiologist for his contributions on the science and to Emily who tried to clean up my questionable grammar, as always any mistakes are entirely my own.

TABLE OF CONTENTS

Foreword   11

IIntroduction   13

On Rubber Balls and Walnuts   15

Part One

The Influences   19
The X-Files as a Grail Myth   *19*
Sumeria's Gilgamesh and Enkidu   *20*
The Twisted Archetypes   *20*

The Players   23
Fox Mulder   *23*
Dana Scully   *25*
William   *26*
Cigarette-Smoking Man (C.G.B. Spender)   *26*
Alex Krycek   *27*

The Aliens.   29
The Black Oil   *29*
The Walk-Ins   *29*
The Rebels   *30*
The Colonists   *30*
The Super Soldiers   *30*
The Alien Replicants   *31*
The Virus   *31*
The Spaceships   *31*
The Lie   *31*

Part Two

TheNames   35

The Episodes - Season One   39
The Pilot   *39*
Deep Throat   *41*
Conduit   *43*
Fallen Angel   *44*
Eve   *45*
E.B.E   *46*
The Erlenmeyer Flask   *46*

The Episodes - Season Two   49
  Little Green Men   49
  Blood   51
  Sleepless   51
  Duane Barry   53
  Ascension   54
  One Breath   55
  Red Museum   56
  Colony   58
  End Game   60
  Fearful Symmetry   62
  F. emasculata   63
  Soft Light   64
  Anasazi   65

The Episodes Season - Three   67
  The Blessing Way   67
  Paper Clip   70
  Nisei   71
  731   72
  Piper Maru   73
  Apocrypha   75
  Jose Chung's From Outer Space   76
  Wetwired   77
  Talitha Cumi   78

The Episodes - Season Four   81
  Herrenvolk   81
  Musings of a Cigarette-Smoking Man   83
  Tunguska   83
  Terma   85
  Never Again   86
  Memento Mori   87
  Tempus Fugit   89
  Max   90
  Zero Sum   91
  Demons   92
  Gethsemane   93

The Episodes - Season Five & Movie   95
  Redux   95
  Redux II   97
  Christmas Carol   98
  Emily   100
  Post-Modern Prometheus   101
  Bad Blood   102
  Patient X   104

The Red and the Black 106
Travelers 107
The End 108
The First Theatrical Movie 111

The Episodes - Season Six 115
The Beginning 115
Triangle 117
Dreamland I & II 119
The Rain King 121
How the Ghosts Stole Christmas 122
S.R. 819. 124
Two Fathers 125
One Son 127
The Unnatural 129
Field Trip 130
Biogenesis 131

The Episodes - Season Seven 135
The 6th Extinction 135
The 6th Extinction - Amor Fati 136
Sein Und Zeit 139
Closure 140
En Ami 141
all things 142
Je Souhaite 143
Requiem 144

The Episodes - Season Eight 147
Within 147
Without 149
Per Manum 150
This Is Not Happening 152
DeadAlive 153
Three Words 154
Vienen 155
Essence 156
Existence 157

The Episodes - Season Nine 161
Nothing Important Happened Today I 161
Nothing Important Happened Today II 162
TrustNo1 163
Provenance 164
Providence 165
William 166

The Truth   167

The Conclusion   173

Bibliography   176

FOREWORD

The fall of 1993 saw the debut of a new sci-fi show from Ten-Thirteen Productions and FOX called *The X-Files*. The series centers on the investigations into the paranormal by two maverick FBI agents, the credulous and impetuous Fox Mulder and the skeptical and cerebral Dana Scully. Before long a narrative thread of mytharc episodes of secret government conspiracies and alien invaders began to weave its way through the various and sundry monsters of the week. The show touched a nerve and became a cult hit. Around water coolers and on the internet heated debates were waged on subjects as diverse as the romantic possibilities between the agents to in-depth theorizing about the conspiracy angle and the aliens. The *Myth-X* analysis was born and fostered in that environment and took shape over all nine seasons. It is only one of myriad possible interpretations of the show and it focuses on the mythic nature of the ongoing mytharc narrative. There are probably as many interpretations of this series' narrative as there are viewers.

From this analysis' point-of-view the series' narrative incorporates science and myth in a marriage that uses each to shine light upon the other. Given Chris Carter's acknowledgement of Joseph Campbell's influences on the show, it focuses on the Jungian mythological viewpoint . Obviously it is not intended to be a comprehensive discussion of myth itself or how things work in the real world. Since the primary focus of this work is to attempt to understand the show's mytharc, it is limited to discussing both science (or at least what passes as science in *The X-Files'* universe) and myth from within the context of its use within this particular narrative. *The X-Files* is science *fiction* after all.

The X-Files is an epic tale rife with Jungian mythical archetypes and metaphorical imagery used to tell a contemporary myth utilizing classic mythological themes. In this story the cast of characters comes from the sub-atomic world of quantum mechanics, plague viruses, shadowy government conspiracies, genetic engineering, and the FBI, all areas of distrust and fear for mankind in the latter part of the 20th century and generally the province of the knowledgeable few.

In this analysis myth refers to the oral or written tales that are used to teach collective cultural beliefs and universal human truths by way of metaphor and symbolism; this is Carl Jung's and Joseph Campbell's myth of the psyche versus the standard Hollywood action/adventure tale. The more common basic adventure story may have an easily understood surface meaning, or the intention may simply be to entertain. While myths can certainly be entertaining, and often use adventure as a storytelling device, the real power is myth's ability to illuminate the human condition. According to Jung, mythic narratives are aimed at the subconscious mind. The mythmaker, using familiar patterns and symbols, serves important psychological needs. The myth may function to help the audience incorporate collective community beliefs, to work though a common personal fear, and/or to illustrate a rite of passage and transformation. For this reason, myths are usually written for a specific cultural group and time, and give voice to their biases and beliefs. A myth's relevance and impact is best viewed against this backdrop. Sometimes, even the most positive myth's power can become dangerous and destructive if its message is held onto and misinterpreted outside of this context. For these reasons, myths have the capacity to be powerful stories that resonate with their audience on a conscious and subconscious level. Cultural groups in every generation create their own mythologies that seek to explain their world in terms that they can understand. Movies like *Star Wars*, *The Matrix*, *ET: the Extra-Terrestrial*, *The Lord of the Rings*, and *Harry Potter*, along with TV shows like *Star Trek* and the new *Battlestar Galactica* are some of the myths for our times.

During the series run, *The X-Files* certainly pushed a few buttons with the viewing public both in America and in other countries. *The X-Files* debut coincided with the rapid proliferation of the internet. The series had a strong online fan base from the beginning, yet a common complaint voiced by this community is that *The X-Files* mytharc doesn't make cohesive sense; it does, just not on the level typically expected from a TV show. With this in mind, Chris Carter's narrative can truly be called mythic. Recognizing the show's mythology can help to assemble the pieces of this complex narrative into a recognizable whole; this analysis and deconstruction is for those viewers who wish to explore the mythological underpinnings for a phenomenal series that raises the bar for televised storytelling.

INTRODUCTION

Myths often try to answer the age old question of creation and/or cultural genesis and the backbone of mythology is the capricious and frightening gods and goddesses to which mankind have attributed all nature of things and events. The mysterious mythological divine world harbors the great unknown that cultural groups have tried for millennia to explain and personalize. *The X-Files* is no exception. As in most creation myths, the gods in this story brought about creation of not only man, but of all living things. They're just not who the viewer or even *X-Files'* characters generally believe them to be nor do they behave in a singular and strictly benevolent manner that a predominantly Judeo/ Christian western culture has come to expect. In *The X-Files'* world, this divine aspect is represented by the various aliens in all of their guises, from the stiletto-wielding alien bounty hunters, the terrorist Rebels, the deal-spinning Colonists to the protective and guiding Walk-Ins. In the typical manner of mythological gods, the aliens run the gamut from the benevolent to the destructive; this divine aspect both torments and guides our heroes Mulder and Scully and shapes their shared destiny.

In *The X-Files'* universe, some of these gods are found in the very small; in their mastery of the world at the molecular and atomic level they hold the most powerful apple on the tree of knowledge. By affecting matter directly, these aliens can create and use radiation as a defense mechanism, repair and replicate from biomaterial or metal, exist in corporeal form or as pure energy, use and animate black oil as a virus, cloak their spaceships, and operate outside of time. Add in their penchant for genetic engineering and they are the ultimate creators and destroyers, the true providence of the mythic divine.

Fox Mulder has devoted his life to finding proof of the paranormal. What he and Scully actually find is a virus; a vessel for the alien sentience and blueprint for their genetic code. The virus carries genetically engineered DNA (oddly enough, not RNA which is what a virus generally uses) that is utilized to pass this sentience on along with the instructions on how to interact with the new host, whether that's by becoming a parasitic puppet master, a beneficial partner, or a transforming reengineer.

Creation myths abound with the archetypal idea of Mother Earth and Father Sky uniting to create life. One could easily see the mythic notion of the sky inseminating the earth and the earth incubating life in its womb as metaphors for *The X-Files'* alien virus which in the narrative's universe came to earth along with the basic building blocks of life in the form of a meteor and then genetically gestated until it spawned life in the distant pass. Most of the virus remains in this metaphorical earth mother suspended in the black oil; even the aliens' mysterious spaceships are often buried underground or submerged in the ocean, harbored by that from which they came.

Chris Carter built *The X-Files'* story and characters around many universal archetypes, not just Mother Earth and Father Sky. *The X-Files'* narrative correlates existing classic mythic metaphors and symbols with new ones that better fit our times. For example, in the aliens mastery of the quantum world, the divine reflects one of the great unknowns that mankind is currently trying to come to grips with. Familiar mythic events–Mulder's resurrection or the star over William's birthplace–are presented in a context that while perhaps less mystical are no less mysterious than their mythological counterparts in the Christian bible. While the archetypes may be manifested in more tangible ways they remain closely tied to their more familiar and inscrutable mythological roles. The aliens as gods play the divine role of creation and determination of fate; yet their knowledge and experience are very different from our own and for the most part unfathomable to mankind.

Oddly enough, even having experienced the viruses' effect personally, this truth is something that neither Mulder nor Scully ever seem to fully grasp or at least remember from one episode to the next. For them, as for the viewer, the aliens' agendas and true natures remain ambiguous and inscrutable and thus frightening. Then again, maybe that's the point; the divine no matter what form it may take is unknowable and fate and destiny are ultimately unchangeable no matter how hard one might struggle against it. In the end, perhaps there is only one true choice: *To love and accept and be redeemed or to hate and exclude and be destroyed.*

While Mulder and Scully's journey is told in archetypal culture hero terms, the righteousness of the quest is ultimately called into question. Mulder and Scully certainly have a destiny to fulfill; however, is it what they believe it to be? Do they in their blind passion to uncover some unknowable truth miss the real point? It is the central conflict which is hinted at throughout the series, but only becomes apparent in the series finale.

As is generally true with any culture hero myth, this one revolves around the battle between good and evil. The evil aspect, however, isn't represented by the aliens; it is manifested in the self-serving and manipulative shadow government called the Syndicate or Consortium and the work of the Project. Just as the true righteousness of the heroes actions is questionable, so too is the very evilness of the villains, nothing is ever black and white on this show. Two of the defining features of *The X-Files'* writing are ambiguity and contradiction which can wreak havoc with attempts to nail down what is happening in any literal kind of way. For the most part the viewer has to rely on inference to figure out how the characters are all connected to each other and what their agendas are. The viewer can buy into the same evil alien story that the Consortium sells Mulder and Scully or he/she can choose to trust no one and evaluate the narrative evidence for themselves. The best way to uncover the real truth is to analyze each mytharc episode in the order in which they were originally aired. In addition, there are several monsters of the week episodes that are beneficial to view as independent metaphorical fairy tales that support and help illuminate the underlying mythic truth.

ON RUBBER BALLS AND WALNUTS

The X-Files narrative is written to have several layers, with the possibility of being enjoyed or to frustrate on many different levels. *The X-Files* narrative can be broken down into a simple allegory of a green rubber ball versus a walnut. I know it sounds strange but bear with me.

At one end of the narrative spectrum there are those viewers who want nothing more than an entertaining diversion or the metaphorical green rubber ball. The rubber ball or narrative is entirely made up of what they see on the surface. There are neither layers to be peeled away nor a central meaty core to be exposed. It is a perfectly legitimate manner in which to enjoy the story and one that doesn't require a whole lot of effort or thought; this is Chris Carter's "scary story".

At the other end of the narrative spectrum is the walnut. From the outside, the walnut doesn't appear to be much different than the green rubber ball. However, instead of being merely an entertaining toy, the walnut is a food that satisfies an important craving. In order to get at that meat, however, one has to break through the outer green rind and the hard shell, something that is not necessarily apparent from the walnut's outward appearance and requires quite a bit of work. Under the green skin there is a hard walnut shell representing the evil alien bad guys or the romance novel love story aspects of the narrative. It now looks like a walnut, but the viewer is still not down to the real meat of the story although a picture is starting to form.

Inside the shell is a treat that equates with the ending of the eighth season finale "Existence." Not everyone likes walnuts however, so the wonderfulness of this treat is relative. If left to continue its development the walnut changes yet again into something else. It begins to sprout, leaving the meat inedible and in a sense spoiled for the short-term; an apt metaphor for the ninth season with its many disappointments. However, long-term the sprout becomes a tree which produces *lots* of walnuts, just as the ninth season narrative sets up the possibility of more stories and another hero cycle.

Of course, as with any spectrum, there is a large gray area in between. Some folks know that there may be a walnut under the skin, but really prefer rubber balls and are completely content using it that way. Some peel away the green rind and find a pecan instead of a walnut, which suits them just fine. Others find the walnut shell beautiful just the way it is and have no interest in the walnut meat. Finally there are those who no matter how much they may want the walnut, can not believe that it was ever created as anything beyond a rubber ball and for them that's all it will ever be.

PART ONE
THE BASICS

THE INFLUENCES

THE X-FILES AS A GRAIL MYTH

The X-Files is not a direct retelling of any one myth; instead it pulls themes and imagery from a variety of sources. The Grail mythology's influence may not be as obvious as the various allusions to the Judeo/Christian myths, but it is no less important to the overall meaning of the narrative.

At its heart *The X-Files* mytharc story is two-fold. First it is the story of the war between titanic races that battle over stewardship of the Earth, the divine retreats from the world and mankind causing a state of decay. Next is the story told using allegorical references to familiar narratives like the Judeo/Christian mythology and the Arthurian Romance of the search for the Grail where a hero is born who must rescue and reunite this primordial power with the world and transform it back to its former glory. It is essentially a quest for the spiritual return of wholeness and balance.

In both the non-Christianized and Christianized versions the search for the Grail is really about restoration and succession in kingship. It is about the journey of the hero archetype to become the king, and not just any king, but the one who will become caretaker of the Grail; a mysterious power that is the source of many wondrous things.

The X-Files' character of Teena Mulder fits well with the Grail narrative's mother archetype who wants to keep her son ignorant of the ways of the knights and who dies after he leaves her to follow that path anyway.

In the series finale, "The Truth", Mulder and Scully find their way to the Grail castle in the form of the Anasazi ruins and find the Fisher King in the frail

Cigarette-Smoking Man. However, they fail to ask the right question, instead focusing on the date of colonization instead of the *nature* of the aliens. The Grail castle and the Fisher King are destroyed and the world is not healed.

SUMERIA'S GILGAMESH AND ENKIDU

There are also aspects of the Sumerian hero epic Gilgamesh interwoven into *The X-Files'* monomyth especially in regards to the partnership between Gilgamesh and Enkidu and the partnership between Mulder and Scully. Like Gilgamesh Mulder is considered a loose cannon before meeting Scully and requires a tempering influence. Not that he isn't still a loose cannon after meeting Scully, but she does control his tendencies a bit, just as Enkidu tempers Gilgamesh's disruptive behavior.

Like Scully, Enkidu is originally intended to occupy Gilgamesh's energies and redirect them onto a more acceptable path by being a challenging combatant. Enkidu began as an innocent wild man who is seduced by a well-meaning prostitute into humanity. One could see the x-file cases as seducing Scully from her innocence in the form of a firm belief in science and the government's good intentions into knowledge of the supernatural and the conspiracy. Like Enkidu, Scully loses her connection to her previous compatriots; for Enkidu it is the animals, for Scully, her fellow agents and scientists. In Enkidu, the gods find the perfect match for Gilgamesh, just like Mulder finds in Scully. Scully's skepticism is a perfect foil for Mulder's credulity.

When Gilgamesh and Enkidu originally clash in a wrestling match, Enkidu wins. He, however, finds respect for Gilgamesh and acknowledges his uniqueness and tells him that he (Gilgamesh) is destined to be king; this has a definite parallel in Scully's willingness to follow Mulder and believe in his kingship as the one.

The end of the Gilgamesh/Enkidu partnership is an interesting parallel too. Basically Enkidu begins to long for his old life just as Scully begins to pine for a normal one and Gilgamesh's answer is to find yet another adventure for them. Unfortunately, the adventure that Gilgamesh devises ultimately kills Enkidu, just as Mulder's inability to give up adventure endangers Scully.

In the end, Gilgamesh fails in his quest for eternal life; instead he achieves self-awareness and a certain amount of acceptance in his mortality. Mulder achieves the same sort of epiphany at the end of "The Truth."

THE TWISTED ARCHETYPES

The writers do a good job literalizing the classic hero's journey in modern terms bringing the fears and unknown into a more modern context–governmental conspiracy and the divine as aliens, respectively without sacrificing the spirit of the classic archetypes. Scully is the sexless Madonna and Mulder is the classic overly arrogant hero out to save the world. However, in true *The X-Files* fashion the writers also turn the archetypes on their heads and they don't ultimately work the way they're supposed to; the hero doesn't save the world or even learn some great unknown that he then shares with the rest of the world–in fact, he pretty much ends up as clueless as he starts out. Sure he comes to believe in something greater than the aliens although he never does figure out that they're basically two sides of the same coin. He also chooses to blatantly ignore what the divine is trying to tell him even though he believes it can save them. He abhors betrayal, yet he himself betrays Scully in the most basic of ways–both with Diana and by abandoning her in season nine–exactly the way his mother and father betray each other. For a man who spent a major portion of his life desperately trying to restore the family that he lost as a child, he certainly loses no time getting out of Dodge once he has it again. He fights against the tyranny of the Consortium, yet in the end does *exactly* the same thing they do by withholding vital information. He fights for the underdog and those on the fringes of society, yet he lumps all of the aliens together as a destructive force that must be destroyed based on the actions of a few and he's as dismissive of those with convictions he doesn't agree with as society itself is of those he champions. He constantly pushes Scully to open her mind to extreme possibilities yet his is closed to anything that doesn't fit his world view.

As the mother archetype, Scully is frequently identified with the Virgin Mary, yet she gives up her desperately wanted child. It's billed as an act of great love, but given the narrative logic that is built up about the omnipotence of the super soldiers and the whole idea that William can only fulfill his destiny if he remains with Mulder it instead becomes incredibly foolish and selfish. The Virgin Mary has to accept Christ's role and support it, not try to second guess the divine and circumvent it or the myth's hero fails. Scully values empirical logic and scientific reasoning, yet in the end she seems to have completely forgotten how to do either. In "Amor Fati" Mulder's dream Scully calls him on his traitorous behavior, yet the real Scully in "The Truth" pacifies his guilt instead of helping him learn from it.

In the end Mulder's no Christ and Scully is no Virgin Mary. Regardless of who it hurts, Mulder wants to be on a cross he has no business being on and Scully wants to be Starbuck to Mulder's Ahab no matter what the cost. Mulder has no interest in actually being a father and Scully doesn't push Mulder to find his true path. Neither really gets the point and does the right thing, something with perhaps less outward glory, but ultimately much more meaning and the true boon in William and what he represents is forever lost to them. The ultimate point seems to be that self-aggrandizing and sacrificing hero trips aren't nearly as important as what normal folks do everyday. When it comes right down to it the more fruitful path–spending one's energy and time raising a child who can understand the importance of harmony and balance between peoples (be that human or alien) and who will perhaps grow up to be the conduit for peaceful coexistence instead of running around in an obviously futile attempt to destroy that which one doesn't understand.

2

THE PLAYERS

FOX MULDER

Special Agent Fox Mulder is an Oxford educated psychologist who is recruited by the FBI as a behavioral profiler where he distinguishes himself as a golden boy. His success allows him to pursue his true passion, the x-files; abandoned unsolved cases of the paranormal.

His interest in the x-files is initially sparked through regression hypnosis of the events surrounding the disappearance of his eight-year old sister when he is twelve and to his exposure to a neurological gas in "The Unusual Suspects." The hypnosis is suggested by Diana Fowley, most likely under the direction of Mulder's arch nemesis and biological father known for most of the series as simply Cigarette-Smoking Man (CSM) and later as

C.G.B. Spender. He manipulates Mulder throughout his life in order to create in him that which he is unable to become himself. Mulder's interest in the paranormal, especially that which pertains to the secret existence of intelligent extraterrestrial life, is necessary in the overall agenda of the Consortium and the fulfillment of Mulder's apparent preordained role in the prophecy that outlines the coming alien colonization.

From a mythological perspective the Fox Mulder character wears several masks throughout the run of the series. All of these roles pertain in some way to the culture hero; it is, after all, his quest and journey that fuels the narrative. Mulder is always identified with mythological characters that in some way affect a transformation, whether that's a dying/resurrecting deity like Jesus; the Holy Grail's Parsifal; or the Navajo's Monster Slayer.

There is a contemporary desire and tendency to want to see our heroes as white hat kind of guys; always righteous and ultimately winning the race. However limiting the character of Fox Mulder to only those terms makes it difficult to really understand *The X-Files'* mytharc. His quest it is not necessarily righteous and because of that he doesn't ultimately win the race. That failure to understand the real truth in favor of clinging to his narrow view of the world is where the real meaning of the narrative lies. In the end, Mulder fails to make the final transformation he is divinely preordained to achieve and his son William is lost to him. That's not to say that Mulder is a bad guy, he's not; but like many classic heroes he falls victim to his own hubris and like many heroes' stories his failure points out a universal human folly.

The writers appear to closely identify Mulder with Christian culture hero Christ through parallel events, most notably crucifixion and resurrection, and associated imagery. Jung associates Christ with the transformation archetype trickster; the alchemic force that causes change. The characterization of Mulder as someone who operates outside of the status quo, his secretiveness, the notorious ditching, the tendency for his actions to backfire on him, the perception by his peers that he is a bit odd or foolish, his hyper-sexuality through innuendo and his preoccupation with pornography; even his often jerky behavior and attitude are all part of his role as the trickster. The twist here is that no matter how much Mulder may want to be the messiah, in the end it is not his destiny to fulfill. Unfortunately like CSM, Mulder's hubris does not allow him to relinquish the destiny he wants for the one the divine have chosen for him and in the ninth season opening episode "Nothing Important Happened Today I" and the series finale "The Truth," he plants his feet firmly on the path to becoming a destroyer and abandons his opportunity to be a healer.

In another analogous trickster parallel; in the fifth season episode "Patient X" CSM refers to Mulder as one of two Navajo warrior twins, most probably the dominant Monster Slayer. On the surface it's an odd identification only in that CSM apparently equates his other son, Jeffrey Spender, with the subservient twin Child of Water (or Born of Water) when instead the characterization of Dana Scully is a far more apt parallel. However, this too is a clue that CSM's worldview is distorted and ultimately incorrect. From CSM's point of view, Mulder's destiny as Monster Slayer is to rid the world of monsters which he believes to be the aliens, when instead *he* is the monster himself. In the series finale "The Truth" Mulder characterizes his quest as chasing monsters with a butterfly net, highlighting one final time his apparent inability to truly grasp the real truth.

Finally, in the third season episode "Quagmire", Scully likens Mulder to Captain Ahab from Melville's *Moby Dick*. While at first it appears to be an overly harsh comparison, given the outcome of Mulder's single-minded quest and his perception of the aliens as evil, it is a fair one. Mulder's aliens are only evil because he believes them to be. Like Captain Ahab out to exact vengeance on Moby Dick for his lost leg, Mulder seeks to destroy that which hurt him as a child. On one hand Mulder sees the literal peg leg as a means of escaping his quest, whereas it is the metaphorical one–the loss of Samantha–that fuels it.

DANA SCULLY

Special Agent Dana Scully is a medical doctor and forensic pathologist who is recruited out of medical school by the FBI. She teaches at the Academy for two years prior to joining Mulder. Scully is assigned to the x-files and instructed to apply her scientific knowledge to his theories. She is never meant to win Mulder's heart; in fact, she's the exact opposite of Mulder's usual romantic type. Instead, she is intended to compliment his various strengths. The fact that she's female is probably originally beside the point to the Consortium. However, the female aspect is vitally important from a mythological point of view. Her scientific mind, honesty, loyalty and steadfastness are also vital, as well as her ability to put aside personal feelings–not her sex appeal. The Consortium wants Mulder connected to her emotionally so that she can be used as a carrot whenever necessary, but not so much that it will sidetrack him or endanger their plans for his future.

In mythological terms the character of Dana Scully is generally identified with the good side of the mother archetype and the goddess, most often in the form of the Virgin Mary. She undergoes her version of the Annunciation in the seventh season episode "all things" and subsequently gives birth in the eighth season finale "Existence" to the messianic child that personifies the duality of the divine and human. Scully's mythology is one of fertility and creation.

Scully is also identified with Judas in two separate episodes; the seventh season "Amor Fati" where she plays the role that Martin Scorsese gives to Judas in *The Last Temptation of Christ* and in the seventh season finale "Requiem" in her placement in the last supper imagery. Judas is an apt parallel; he is the most important of the apostles in the fulfillment of Christ's destiny. Without Judas' betrayal, the crucifixion would never happen. Scully doesn't actively betray Mulder, but she does play the role of the one who pushes him towards his true destiny. There is a dichotomy here in that Scully also plays the tempering role that first mate Starbuck plays with Captain Ahab. It's up to Scully to ask the hard questions–especially the ethical ones. At times she tries to get Mulder to at least consider the option of getting out of the car.

Scully also plays Sir Gawain to Mulder's Sir Percival in *The X-Files* version of the Grail myth and the Child of Water twin to Mulder's Monster Slayer. Scully may not be a sidekick, but she definitely plays the subservient role to Mulder's heroic one. That doesn't make Scully any less of a hero however, since she is ultimately the one who conceives, carries, and nurtures the messianic child. She is also the one who has to make the heartbreaking decision to let him go.

In her medical and spiritual personas, Scully also plays a shaman of sorts or a conduit to the divine. While not as obvious as the third season's Navajo Albert Hosteen, she too is closely in tune with the divine. There is a great deal of irony in the fact that the skeptic is the one most often visited by the various spirit guides.

Scully isn't perfect, she is closed-minded, possessive, and insecure. She is as guilty of failing William's destiny as Mulder is. Like Mulder, Scully wants to believe; quickly buying into the theory that best fits her scientific and/or Catholic bias, even to the point of ignoring evidence.

WILLIAM

William is the third generation hero. His destiny belongs to the Walk-Ins. He is not an abomination like the alien Project babies and is a full integration of the divine and man; the new biogenesis of a new species, not a hybrid with a dual nature. There is no struggle for control within him because there is only one sentience. William represents the fully transfigured messianic figure that will save halves from extinction.

CIGARETTE-SMOKING MAN (C.G.B. SPENDER)

On *The X-Files*, culture hero CSM is Darth Vadar to Mulder's Anakin Skywalker; they are not so much two sides of the same coin as they are illustrations of different stages of the same hero journey. Generally hero cycles require the hero to triumph over and replace the king whose fading potency is draining the land of vitality. Some heroes become conquerors in a negative way, as CSM does and as Mulder is on his way to becoming after his decision to leave in "Nothing Important Happened Today I" and in his continuing obsession to follow a meaningless quest in "The Truth." At every hero's crossroads there are two paths from which to choose, the one that leads from embracing the mythic truth and the one that leads from ignoring it. At the end of the former lies glory and transformation into the divine and a healing and creative power, at the end of the latter lies infamy and the transformation into the monster and a destructive power.

CSM, not Bill Mulder, is Mulder's biological father. In the Navajo warrior twin mythology, the twins' mother Changing Woman misidentifies their father in an attempt to discourage them from seeking out their true one–the sun. On the show, Teena Mulder hides Mulder's true paternity from him in a futile attempt to keep him from following in his father's footsteps.

From the Grail mythology standpoint, CSM represents the Fisher King; the wounded king who is turning the world into a wasteland. In "The Truth", CSM sits in his Grail castle of Anasazi ruins in the middle of a barren desert awaiting Mulder's arrival and the question that by its asking would heal the world. Unfortunately Mulder doesn't ask it–what is the true nature of the aliens and colonization–and the Fisher King is destroyed. Instead Mulder does take up the crown; however, in his focus on the date of colonization as a date of extinction instead of transformation and rebirth, he becomes the next wounded Fisher King who must await *his* son's own journey for his own healing.

ALEX KRYCEK

Alex Krycek represents the shadow of Fox Mulder and to a lesser degree Walter Skinner. He embodies all the qualities of Mulder's darker nature, violence, vengeance, disloyalty, and betrayal. He's not Mulder's opposite–that's Scully–because all of these qualities show up periodically in Mulder when his darker nature comes to the forefront.

In his identification with Kundry from the Grail mythology, Krycek also frequently represents the force that keeps Mulder on his quest; the kiss in "The Red and the Black" is a nice play on that association. Since Krycek also personifies Mulder's shadow, it's his use as the prod that keeps Mulder chasing aliens which signifies that it's Mulder's darker and negative nature that underlies his quest. An idea that is also illustrated by Krycek's focus on destroying the real truth disguised as a heroic attempt to destroy the aliens.

Krycek often tries to become the king by grabbing the king's power–in stealing the MJ data tape in "Paper Clip", in his attempt to kill CSM in "Requiem", and in his tendency to play one side against the other just as CSM does. He wants to be the favored son and heir, something he can never achieve. In a way, Krycek, not Mulder, is the bastard son and these attempts at legitimacy always fail. In "DeadAlive" Krycek, like the Pharaoh and King Herod, wants to kill William before he's even born in order to destroy a potential rival for kingship. He is also instrumental in Scully's abduction (but not her return) in the second season episode "Ascension" since as William's mother; Scully also represents a serious threat to Krycek's bid to be king.

In the end, it is Skinner, not Mulder, who faces the shadow and destroys it by shooting Krycek, freeing himself from its control. Mulder, on the other hand, remains tied to his darker nature and allows the shadow to continue to call the shots; as seen by Krycek's help in "The Truth." Krycek is the only one of the dead who apparently pushes Mulder to go through with the trial. Krycek and the shadow are finally redeemed when he chooses Marita (who represents love to him) over the need for vengeance and his negative influence on Mulder ends–that alone does not free Mulder; first he must choose love himself and be redeemed too.

THE ALIENS

THE BLACK OIL

The black oil acts as a medium for the two strains of the older alien virus. One strain, the one found in "Tunguska," is the purest form which appears to just want to remain inert in the oil and has no other real agenda. It attempts to call for rescue when its oil field is threatened in "Vienen" or seeks other means of escape if it is otherwise in danger of destruction. It generally does not harm its host unless by events outside of its control and leaves it as soon as it has an opportunity to return to either a ship or the oil. It does *not* seek a human body for permanent occupation and only uses infection as a means to an end. However, at least one strain of the older virus will convert the biomass of a host into a juvenile Gray that will mature if given enough heat. It is not specified if this transformation is intentional or an unwanted and uncontrollable trait. It appears to be spontaneous and may be the original form for the Walk-Ins who have since evolved. Perhaps the actual point of the virus is to create a suitable vessel for the disembodied sentience with whatever material is at hand.

THE WALK-INS

The Walk-Ins represent the divine in the narrative. They want the reintegration of both halves of the whole (alien and human) using natural means; this results in a single sentience allowing a return to physical and spiritual harmony. The Walk-Ins are most often associated with the mysterious spirit guides and the powerful ships, like the ones in "Amor Fati" and "Providence" and in the end with the alien replicants. The Walk-Ins rescue Scully from the Consortium in "One Breath" and return her to Mulder with Nurse Owens watching over her until she makes it back from the other side safe and sound. Cassandra Spender is abducted by the Walk-Ins on various occasions except for her abduction by the Consortium in "Patient X" and her destruction by the Rebels in "One Son." When the Walk-Ins do show up in a corporeal alien form it is as a Gray. The Rebels and Colonists appear to have mostly abandoned this form in favor of the human-like ones with green blood. The Walk-Ins take all of the abductees once William is conceived and change them into alien replicants.

THE REBELS

The Rebels want racial purity and complete separation; they represent the fallen much like Satan does in the Judeo/Christian mythology. Their rebellion is against the Walk-Ins but they are at war with the Colonists. They are the State that the Colonists are working against. They are often associated with the Nazis on the show. They attempt to destroy all the abductees that the Consortium has genetically altered in "Patient X" and "The Red and the Black" and steal the well-spring. They are the aliens with the scarred over faces; a protection tactic used to avoid infection by one of the altered viruses and its impure RNA. They too have the bodies with green blood.

THE COLONISTS

Like the Rebels the Colonists are fallen and are the alien version of the Consortium. While the Consortium wants parasitic human (super soldier) hegemony through artificial hybridization with human sentience control, the Colonists want parasitic alien hegemony through artificial hybridization with alien sentience control. They are working against the Rebels to eradicate their identical natures in a manner not sanctioned by the State. The Gregors and the adult fake Samanthas from "Colony" and "End Game" belong to this faction. These are the deal-makers with the Consortium, both sides appearing to work together to create a hybrid, but conducting their own work on the side to different ends and undermining the deal. Ultimately the Colonists just want to come home and return to grace, they just don't understand how to do it. Their version of the virus resides in toxic green goo that makes up their physical human-like bodies.

THE SUPER SOLDIERS

The super soldiers are the creation of the Consortium's Project and are a combination of alien and human physiology utilizing the best of both. However, it appears as though the super soldiers themselves have their own agenda and are replacing vital people at important positions to gain governmental control. They are not content to be the workhorses of the Consortium and want to take over total control for themselves and they become the new evil. They want William killed or better yet, never born, but if they can't achieve that they want to neutralize Mulder and his all important influence given that William's destiny hinges on this.

THE ALIEN REPLICANTS

The alien replicants are the Walk-Ins version of the Project's super soldiers. They are attempting to create their own army of a sort. The Walk-Ins
allow the abductees own sentience to remain in control until William's birth
when they take over long enough to act as witnesses and protectors. Presumably the humans retake control afterwards and return to their lives.

THE VIRUS

Ultimately the alien sentience is carried in or enabled by the virus, but it
can use various forms – human-like with green blood, black oil, the Grays,
human hosts, and the metal vertebrae to operate. There are various alien bounty
hunters who appear to have special qualities working for the Colonists and the
Rebels and at least one renegade that works for CSM.

On *The X-Files* the aliens not only inhabit the mysterious world of the
divine, in a marriage of science and myth, they also operate in the equally
mysterious world of the quantum or Samantha's starlight; *The X-Files* version
of a sun god myth.

The aliens' group sentience or the mythic representation of Jung's collective unconscious has the ability to control and manipulate sub-atomic particles,
gravity, and space-time. Mastery of matter at the quantum and molecular level
allows the aliens to create and use radiation as a defense mechanism, use a virus
and bacteria as a means of introducing their sentience and divine plan into
another organism in the form of DNA, the ability to rearrange and transform
biological material from one form to another, and to use carbon in the form of
petroleum as a protective medium and means of transportation into a suitable
host.

THE SPACESHIPS

The spaceships–both triangular and round–demonstrate via bright light,
self-repair, radiation, electronic interference, and the ability to operate outside
of the laws of gravity and time, that the aliens can affect the macro world,
which abide by the laws of relativity. Even the aliens' vulnerability to magnetite is related to their quantum nature.

THE LIE

In *The X-Files'* universe intimate knowledge and mastery of the quantum
world represents the ultimate apple on the tree of knowledge. The misuse of
that knowledge by the Consortium and military through the use of alien technology is the source of the evil that befalls our heroes and mankind.

The viewer is given several strong suggestions that all is not what it seems
in Mulder and Scully's world. Michael Kritschgau lays it all out very nicely in
the fourth season finale episode "Gethsemane" his only error is in assuming

that there are no aliens at all. There are, they are just not at all like what Mulder and Scully are led to believe. Instead the Consortium rigs things and uses mind altering drugs and/or devices to control Mulder's and other abductees' beliefs so that the aliens become the bad guy. It is obvious that there are even members of their own ranks who have bought the lie, hook, line and sinker; Well-Manicured Man and Alex Krycek are prime examples.

The first season opening episode "Deep Throat" and the sixth season "Dreamland" arc show that the military has access to and the use of alien technology all the way to the ability to fly and presumably use the spaceships. In "Jose Chung's from Outer Space" it is clear that at least some of the so-called alien abductions are staged and the subjects' memories of the tests performed skewed via hypnosis or drugs. It is also clear that there are aliens, but that they are significantly different in nature than the viewers' have been led to expect. Lord Kinebote, while frightening is actually benevolent in nature.

It is possible that the nefarious abductions and tests are mostly the work of the Consortium. That's not to say that there are no true alien abductions on the show. The question is which are which and what are the true purposes of both. Cassandra has very positive recollections from her previous abductions; memories which suggests an alien race who has returned to heal the world. It isn't until her abduction in "Patient X" that she has a negative experience; this suggests that at least one faction of the aliens is benevolent from mankind's point of view.

In "The Unusual Suspects" Mulder is sprayed with a substance that seems to either start or intensify his belief in extraterrestrials. His subsequent regression hypnosis therapy may only add to his inaccurate memory of what transpires the night Samantha is taken. His dream recollections in "Demons" may be the accurate ones; Cigarette-Smoking Man comes to the house to get Samantha and Teena fights it. Mulder is then implanted with the false memories of an alien abduction in order to start him down the road that the Consortium needs him on; namely to loudly accuse the Consortium of hiding the existence of extraterrestrials and the idea of the colonization threat thus adding to the alien mystique.

PART TWO

THE DETAILS

4

THE NAMES

Since the Ten-Thirteen writers always leave character motivation extremely vague and ambiguous the viewer has to look for clues anywhere they can in order to discern just what any particular character's ultimate agenda might be.

The fact that many of the Consortium members typically remain nameless suggests that names have symbolic importance. Some names are reused frequently on *The X-Files* and seem to denote specific meanings to their owners (e.g., William) and that seems to be born out when analyzing them.

Dana Katherine Scully–Dana means mother of the gods. Since "God" on *The X-Files* is synonymous with alien this is probably a nod to her role as mother of William. That's not to say that William is an alien–but that he is the final culmination of the mingling of alien and human DNA and the birth of a new evolutionary branch that will benefit both sides. His role as the messianic figure in the myth also suggests a certain connection to the divine. Katherine means pure and is probably a reference to Scully's frequent identification as a Madonna figure. She is also extremely pure in motive and deed.

Fox William Mulder–Fox traditionally means nothing more than "fox" as in the woodland canine. However, foxes generally suggest cleverness, slyness, sneakiness, etc. which describes Mulder fairly well and is also a nod to his archetypal role as the trickster. He is extremely intelligent, very clever and he is sneaky and sly–he frequently holds back information and often pulls fast ones. William is a powerful name on the show and is reused often; it means determined protector. It also fits Mulder and is probably a big clue about his son's ultimate role. His father is a William too–as is Scully's–and while on the surface Bill Mulder didn't appear to fit the bill, his motivation was protection even if his chosen methods are faulty. Scully's brother also carries this name and is usually portrayed as over-protective. Not to mention that Billy is a form of William; which also casts Billy Miles in the protector light.

Samantha Ann Mulder–Samantha means God heard, perhaps a reference to how she is rescued by the Walk-Ins. Ann means favored grace which may refer to some specialness–or grace–that she had. In many ways, Samantha was the forerunner to William; she plays the same role in Bill Mulder's journey as William does in Mulder's.

Walter Sergei Skinner–Walter means powerful ruler or powerful warrior and both definitions fit Skinner fairly well. Sergei is the Russian form of Serge, which means servant; an interesting dichotomy that really does describe Skinner. He is in a position of power–and frequently uses it–but he is also very much a servant, in the beginning to the Consortium and ultimately to Krycek due to the nanobots, and in a more positive light–to Mulder and Scully's cause.

John Doggett–John means God is merciful or God's grace. Perhaps Doggett was sent by the Walk-Ins to help Scully during her time of need; in which case it suggests that the Walk-Ins are merciful. In the Judeo/Christian metaphor that has been pervasive throughout the myth, this may also be a reference to the Apostle John.

Monica Reyes–Monica means advisor and she certainly has the tendency to hand out advice, especially on feelings. Reyes often plays the role of wisdom on the show. On a side note—the surname Reyes means descendant of the king's house–is this a reference to her biological history? If so, coupled with her early struggle against smoking, it may be a hint at a genetic connection to CSM (who represents the king archetype). If so, it's a connection that is never played out.

Alex Krycek–interestingly enough Alexander means protector of mankind. Is this a clue about Krycek's true motivations? It could easily be, since it does appear that for the most part he is trying to save humanity even if his methods are questionable. In the end however, he sells out and does not learned the real truth, which means he too fails in the hero role. In fact, he plays the perfect shadow to Mulder–just as Diana does to Scully. Their surface goals may be the same, but their truths are not.

Diana Fowley–again, this one is especially interesting since Diana means divine or goddess. Does this suggest that she–not Scully–is Mulder's goddess on his hero's journey? Or is it a reference to the Greek Goddess Diana who is the huntress? Diana certainly plays the huntress in her dealings with Mulder and she also represents the dark side of the mother and goddess archetypes.

Cassandra Spender–Cassandra means prophet and she certainly plays that part. In fact, she plays the role of John the Baptist in the Judeo/Christian metaphor. Cassandra is also the name of the woman in Greek mythology who is destined by the gods to prophesize but to forever suffer the disbelief of others.

Daniel Waterston–Dana is the feminine form of Daniel and on *The X-Files* she is (or was at least prior to her full indoctrination into the x-files) exactly that. She and Daniel apparently shared similar views on the feasibility of the paranormal–at least until she has her epiphany in "all things." Daniel also means God is my judge–which seems to have been the case. He is dying because he isn't living up to his past sins against his family (there's the connection to the myth–another example of the destruction of family and the results) and until he faces up to it and restores balance he can't live.

5

THE PILOT

The pilot episode of *The X-Files* introduces the show's two protagonists, Special Agents Fox Mulder and Dana Scully to the viewers and to each other. Scully is assigned to work with Mulder by Section Chief Blevins. He is later revealed in the fifth season opening episode arc "Redux" and "Redux II" to be a mole for the Consortium represented in the pilot by a silent and brooding Cigarette-Smoking Man. One of the narrative's overreaching conflicts revolves around Mulder's apparent inability to escape the manipulations of the Consortium, mostly orchestrated by CSM and facilitated by Mulder's own single-minded focus on his so-called truth. When Mulder later tells Scully that nothing else matters to him, he reveals not only his personal perception of his hero's quest but also his greatest weakness.

Mulder begins the series believing Scully to be a spy, planted to keep tabs on him with her little reports. Scully, on the other hand, begins their partnership believing Mulder to be something of a nut job–albeit a brilliant one. Over the course of this first episode, Mulder begins to understand Scully's true agenda, which like his, is to find the truth and Scully begins to understand what motivates Mulder's quirky behavior. A fragile trust is built that grows over the course of the series into a transcendent partnership of mythological proportions a la the Sumerian's Gilgamesh and Enkidu. Their relationship is not your typical trite TV series romance, heavy on sex and lust and short on soul, instead it is of the truly platonic type. On *The X-Files* sex takes on its mythic nature as either a destructive temptation or a world-healing creative power. The Mulder/Scully relationship is divinely preordained; the product of which, their son William, is the real answer to healing the world and the ultimate truth. Does all of this make *The X-Files* just another sappy romance? It can be viewed this way, but on a deeper level this show is about the destructive nature of a single-minded quest. An obsession that precludes the ability to see what's right in front of one's nose regardless of how often the divine points it out and the hubris of blindly believing one's point of view to be the only right one; a powerful message in today's world. At Mulder and Scully's initial meeting, she makes a prophetic observation; *"the answers are there, you just have to know where to look."* Chris Carter's signature use of ambiguity and a narrative open to various interpretations is yet another illustration of this concept.

In the pilot, we get our first taste of Mulder's mysterious extraterrestrials and the narrative's mythic divine. There are neither visible spaceships nor little green men; here they are represented merely as light, a possible early indicator of their mastery of the quantum and much like the quantum world, the only tangible evidence of their existence is the results of their actions; the implants and related nosebleeds; the strange electrical disturbances; missing time; the bumps and organic chemical traces; Ray Soames' transformation and the inexplicable behavior of the abductees. In the first of many myth/science parallels drawn by the writers is the connection between apparent clinical schizophrenic behavior and a divine influence, echoing the early belief that mental illness was a sign of spiritual possession.

Rebirth, one of the prevalent archetypes and reoccurring themes in *The X-Files'*, makes its first tentative appearance in Ray Soames' partial biological transformation after death. Ray's failed transformation is a precursor to the later resurrections, a common manifestation of the rebirth archetype. Even Billy Miles' reawakening from his persistent vegetative state can be seen as a kind of rebirth albeit not as obvious as his eighth season return from the dead as an alien replicant.

In the pilot episode, Mulder's recollection of his sister's abduction is significantly different than his later descriptions of the event; this is a possible clue about the questionable value of memories recovered via regression hypnosis. *The X-Files* frequently uses the phenomenological notion that our bias and expectations color our perception of events. An idea most vividly portrayed in the third season episode "Jose Chung's From Outer Space" where author Jose Chung attempts to deduce the truth about an abduction as seen through various characters' eyes. Mulder begins his journey with an expected outcome—the existence of alien abductors—firmly in place in his mind and he generally dismisses or ignores any evidence to the contrary. His deeply held belief that this outcome is the only true one is an important factor in understanding the underlying theme of the show and the reason why Mulder and Scully never truly achieve resolution. Mulder isn't so much interested in finding out the real truth as he is in proving his version of it. There is an important distinction between the two and CSM frequently uses Mulder's single-mindedness against him. It is easy to sell the evil alien story to Mulder, because it's the one he expects and more importantly wants to hear. Scully originally realizes the folly of this line of thinking, but somewhere along the way, she falls prey to it herself.

Under hypnosis, Billy Miles tells Mulder that the aliens are getting rid of the evidence of a failed experiment. At the end of the seventh season, the Oregon abductees, this time along with Mulder, are reabducted in order to be used as hosts for alien replicants. Since they and Mulder exhibit strange brain activity prior to these abductions, it seems that the initial experiment isn't a complete failure after all. Given that in the fifth season episodes "Patient X" and "The Red and the Black", it is revealed that there is a war taking place between the Colonists and the Rebels, it seems likely. Perhaps the Colonists originally abduct the Oregon teenagers and start a process that in the eighth season produces the replicants. The Rebels may be attempting to forestall that eventuality by destroying the affected abductees in the pilot. The Walk-Ins generally work in much more subtle ways through guidance and not destruction.

At the end of the pilot there is a tribute of a sort to Spielberg's *Raiders of the Lost Ark*. CSM places the recovered implant amongst seemingly thousands of other objects in a room at the center of the Pentagon, apparently catalogued and then forgotten; a strong image of those in power using withheld vital knowledge as a means of control.

DEEP THROAT

The events in the episode "Deep Throat" begin to set the stage for the central conflicts in the mytharc. The two main ideas put forth are that the military has recovered alien technology and is actively retrofitting it for their use and that Mulder is being led around by the nose. A third idea touched upon briefly is that Mulder's quest may not be as righteous as he likes to believe it is. Finally "Deep Throat" also continues to echo the notion that one's experience of reality is tied to one's perceptions when the fake reporter Paul tells Mulder that people see what they want to see. All of these ideas are heavily developed throughout the run of *The X-Files* and eventually come to a fruition of a sort in the series finale "The Truth."

It becomes obvious that the Consortium has been keeping tabs on Mulder for awhile and they set up the Budahas situation in order to entice Mulder to Idaho. Deep Throat showing up and telling Mulder not to go is tantamount to waving a red flag in front of a bull; it certainly isn't going to persuade him to drop it. At this point in time, Mulder's all-important perception is still being shaped, which means that the Consortium have to give him enough proof to develop his belief in the existence of extraterrestrials and the military's involvement, but not enough to hang themselves. They can't give Mulder direct evidence of anything, but they can place subconscious ideas that influence him. Deep Throat is the conduit for fanning these flames and either knowingly or unwittingly isn't quite the benefactor Mulder believes him to be. Mulder eventually comes to believe that Budahas is a decoy. It's more likely that Budahas is bait, which Mulder takes hook, line and sinker.

Mulder's curiosity sets him up for capture at Ellens Air Base, where he undergoes some kind of mind wipe. Given that Mulder only loses those memories that are tied to what he saw at the base, the mind wipe on the surface seems to be overkill. In any case, if the Consortium doesn't want him o see the ship the hanger seems a particularly bad place to take him. It's more likely that he underwent something else between the time he is initially captured and the time he arrives at the hanger and those are the memories that are wiped out.

Scully goes ballistic when she realizes that the military has Mulder. Perhaps Paul shows up specifically to set up Mulder's return and/or test Scully's loyalty. There appears to be no other real reason for him to show up at the motel. Not only does the Consortium need to influence Mulder, they also have to begin preparing Scully. They want her to remain skeptical enough to push Mulder, but wary enough of the government to support him. It's a fine line to walk.

Regardless of the set up, Lieutenant Colonel Budahas does appear to be suffering from a classic case of exposure to alien technology of some kind. He sports the radiation burn rash and is suffering from a psychotic episode and seizures when he is arrested by the MPs. There is no sign of the black oil, so it's unlikely that he's actually harboring an alien presence, it is more likely that he's reacting to sustained exposure to the quantum nature of one of the stolen spaceships.

Mulder's flagrantly displays two of his more irritating habits with regard to his partner– ditching and withholding information. As always both get him into a lot of trouble from which Scully must extract him setting a precedence that lasts throughout the run of the show. Scully's skepticism, on the other hand, is in full bloom, which causes the ditch in the first place; however, Mulder's withholds information for no discernable reason. He does eventually fill her in; unfortunately by this point his behavior has effectively removed Scully's ability to make an informed decision about becoming involved in the case; this is really no different from all the times that the Consortium and Cigarette-Smoking Man control her. Mulder is already starting to become that which he abhors without even realizing it. In "Deep Throat" Mulder voices an important point, *"When do the human costs become too high?"* Given the outcome of his quest perhaps he should have taken that more to heart.

When Deep Throat approaches Mulder at the end of the episode, he tells him that their lives are now in danger. He also voices yet another important idea when he asks Mulder why with all the evidence to the contrary he still believes in extraterrestrials. Mulder's reply, *"because all of the evidence to the contrary is not dissuasive enough"* could be the mantra for the mytharc itself. Regardless of how much evidence there is to the evil nature of the aliens, it is not dissuasive enough in the face of the many narrative contradictions to that conclusion.

CONDUIT

The first season episode "Conduit" plays on three reoccurring themes on *The X-Files*, the difference between perception and reality, the alien/human connection, and most importantly, Samantha's abduction as Mulder's driving force.

Before the whole Consortium/alien hybridization deal muddies the waters of the mytharc, the aliens are much more clearly portrayed as a sort of amoral force interacting with humans in various and not always frightening ways. Mulder still views them with wonder and hasn't yet been fed the evil alien story, which he later buys into wholeheartedly.

In "Conduit" Kevin Morris has a connection to the aliens and in a nod to the movie *Poltergeist* receives messages from the static in TV transmissions in the form of binary numbers. Not only is this an early sign of the possible quantum nature of the aliens, it is also a hint at their desire to connect with humanity in some way. Perhaps Kevin has his junk DNA turned on much as Gibson Praise does albeit in a much more limited way. There is no reason for the aliens to send Kevin this information except to perhaps comfort him with the knowledge that Ruby will be returned, much as Mulder is comforted during Samantha's abduction. In "Conduit" Mulder's regression hypnosis memories of the night Samantha is taken are very different than those he later remembers in dreams. The aliens tell him not to be afraid, that she won't be harmed and that she'll be returned some day. "Conduit" illustrates just how much Samantha's abduction influences Mulder's behavior and desires. On the surface, Mulder appears to be truly concerned about the disappearance of Ruby Morris for her own sake. However, Scully recognizes that what Mulder is really reacting to is his own desire to find Samantha. Ruby is a stand in of sorts, just as Scully later becomes when she too is abducted.

The Walk-Ins even make sure that Kevin knows when and where Ruby will be returned ensure that she can be rescued in time. One point to remember is that this does not indicate that they are the ones who abduct Ruby or Samantha, only that they may be the ones who will ultimately protect them. Unfortunately Samantha isn't returned as Ruby and Scully are; the Walk-Ins find it necessary to take her to keep her from additional harm.

The Walk-Ins' method of communication is interesting in that they've chosen bits of data taken from the Voyager probe's golden record, mankind's original greeting to extraterrestrial life–a tactic they use again later with Mulder in the second season opening episode "Little Green Men." They apparently want to minimize their contact to a chosen few, not surprising given that the military apparently has standing orders to destroy them at any opportunity. Contrast this behavior with that of the NSA who dispassionately run roughshod over the Morris' home and life in a clearly ridiculous effort to pin espionage charges on an eight-year old boy; an early indication of where the true evil lies.

"Conduit" flirts with the idea of the disparity between perception and reality with the light becoming not aliens, but a group of motorcycles, the seemingly random binary numbers becoming a picture of Ruby, and the sheriff's contention that Ruby ran away because of his knowledge of her prior behavior. Even Mulder's inconsistent recounting of Samantha's abduction supports the notion that everything is not always as it seems.

As a trickster culture hero, Mulder is inherently narcissistic and ultimately self-serving. His struggle to overcome his self-obsession and become a part of a whole is the essence of his journey to self-discovery. Unlike Scully, Mulder has no problem with individualization; his issues are with integration and seeing the world outside of his own point of view and influence. For all of Mulder's preaching on the idea of opening a closed mind, he is in fact, the worst offender. Mulder's biggest blind spot and hubris is his belief that his perception is the only reality.

Sometimes these twists in perception are subtle, like the light in the forest in "Conduit" that turns out to be a bunch of motorcycles and the one in the pilot episode that turns out to be Deputy Miles' headlights. Monica Reyes sums it up in the eighth season episode "This is Not Happening" when she tells Scully and Skinner that what we think may have happened may not be what actually did happen.

FALLEN ANGEL

"Fallen Angel" is a difficult episode to reconcile with the mytharc as a whole since its corporeal alien doesn't fit the mold later established. However, Max Fenig's abduction experiences and apparent schizophrenia do fit to a large degree. He has an implant of some kind, although in his case it is imbedded in his cerebellum via an incision behind his left ear. A possession by the alien is painful and causes his ear to bleed—much like the nosebleeds of the Oregon abductees from the pilot episode. Like those same abductees, Max has been diagnosed with schizophrenia. He also has epilepsy, the seizures starting when he is around ten-years old; around the same time as his episode of waking up in a strange place without any memory of how he got there. Both conditions are undoubtedly caused by alien intervention, most likely due to the implant.

The alien in "Fallen Angel" is apparently looking for Max when its spaceship crashes. There is no mention of magnetite at this point and since a recovery craft shows up and does not crash, it is unlikely that The X-Files' form of kryptonite is the cause. A play on the term fallen angel itself may refer to the mythological divine nature of the aliens and the fallen state of the Rebels and Colonists.

The alien spaceship gives off some kind of ionizing radiation, which shows up again in "E.B.E.," "Tempus Fugit"/"Max," "Vienen" and "Provenance"/ "Providence." Here is the first really strong indication of the quantum-like nature of the aliens, as is their ability to cloak and possess Max. The craft appears to be the same as the triangular spaceship from "Deep Throat" and later seen in "Apocrypha," "The Red and the Black," "Biogenesis," "The 6th Extinction," "Amor Fati," "Requiem," "Within," "Without," and "Provenance"/ "Providence."

Max mentions that Mulder has quite a reputation in the alien fanatic circle and that Mulder's written at least one magazine article under the pen name M.F. Luder which may explain the Consortium's ongoing claim that to kill him would start a crusade. "Fallen Angel" reveals that Section Chief McGrath wants the x-files closed down and Mulder fired. As useful as Mulder is, there are limits to what the Consortium will tolerate. However, Deep Throat wants to keep Mulder close so he can keep an eye on him.

In "Fallen Angel" Mulder is behaving in the trickster mode. He is singularly fixated on the crashed ship to the exclusion of everything else, even with the threat of the closure of the x-files hanging over his head. Scully again has to extract him from the mess he's made by doing so. In fact, Scully is the one who is concerned about and fights for the x-files, not Mulder.

EVE

"Eve" is the first episode that deals with the genetically engineered super soldier concept. The Litchfield Project begins in the early 1960s as an answer to Russia's eugenic attempts to create a better soldier. Unfortunately the extra chromosomes of 4, 5, 12, 16, and 22 and the related additional genes cause not only heightened strength and intelligence, but also a deep psychosis that is either suicidal and/or homicidal.

Eve 7 better known as fertility expert Sally Kendrick, attempts to correct the default in two in vitro clones of herself; Tina Simmons and Cindy Reardon who are born and raised 3,000 miles apart. Instead the psychosis begins earlier. The new Eves how signs of telepathy, not only between themselves, but with others not only do both girls exsangunate their fathers at the exact same time Tina Simmons easily manipulates Mulder by playing to his preconceived abduction scenario.

Mulder and Scully's initial theories on what's going on are wrong, it's neither Mulder's alien mutilation nor quite the two serial killers working in tandem scenario that Scully has in mind. Overall Scully's theory is the closer of the two and she actually suspects the girls at one point. Ultimately, while the aliens don't have anything to do with Tina and Cindy, the genetic engineering that goes hand in hand with them does. As is typically the case the real answer falls somewhere in the gray area between the two extreme points of view.

There is a strong suggestion that the Eves are the personification of evil, in the red outfits that Cindy and Tina wear, to the identification of Eve 6 with Thomas Harris' Hannibal Lector. In reality they are merely the product of a more insidious evil in the form of the Project doctors and their work to create a better killing machine.

E.B.E.

The episode "E.B.E." begins the conspiracy theme with the introduction of the Lone Gunmen Melvin Frohike, John Byers, and Ringo (Richard) Langley and the idea that Mulder and Scully are under surveillance by the nefarious "they." Mulder suggests that Gulf War Syndrome may be caused by the use of alien technology during the Gulf War; something the Lone Gunmen find amusing. Given that the episode "Providence" suggests that the super soldiers made an appearance during the Gulf War, perhaps it's not such a bad theory after all.

For all of their power, the aliens and their mysterious triangular ships are still vulnerable to a human missile and apparently a bullet. Deep Throat tells Mulder of an international agreement in place since 1947 that stipulates that any country that captures an extraterrestrial biological entity must destroy it. Like the Fisher King the divine has also been wounded and requires healing, however, mankind in fear chooses to destroy instead of seeking transformation. Deep Throat also tells Mulder of his own experience acting as executioner; how the alien wore an innocent and blank expression—in other words; it is not the monster it is believed to be. It is this experience that leads to Deep Throat's interest and covert support of Mulder's work to reveal the truth. Based on various events throughout the run of the series, it would appear that actions stemming from guilt are not as successful or righteous as those driven by love.

"E.B.E." revisits the idea that time goes missing in the presence of a real alien spaceship. The manipulation of time seems to be the one thing that the government hoaxers can not replicate. In contrast, the bright light and electronic disturbances show up during both the truck driver's initial real encounter and Mulder and Scully's later hoaxed one.

Deep Throat is not above deceiving Mulder when it better suits his agenda to do so. Mulder catches Deep Throat in a lie when he tries to use a fake photo to distract Mulder from following the truck. "E.B.E." underscores the dangers of Mulder trusting others too quickly. For the first (but not only) time Scully tries to get Mulder to see that his blind and overpowering obsession is a vulnerability that the Consortium will take advantage of. Something Mulder falls prey to again and again; even as late as the series finale "The Truth" where Cigarette-Smoking Man plays him one last time.

THE ERLENMEYER FLASK

"The Erlenmeyer Flask" marks the beginning of the revised direction of the mytharc caused by Gillian Anderson's surprise pregnancy. The whole notion of the Consortium and the alien/human hybrids begins to take shape in this episode. The super soldier idea is obliquely suggested and the benefits of hybridization are stressed.

Mulder and Scully find their first evidence of Purity or the alien virus–although it is hinted at previously in the pilot episode. The name Purity itself suggests the aliens' divine nature, as does the name well-spring given to the alien fetus. Dr. Berube is a geneticist who is working on the Human Genome Project the first indication that genetics are somehow involved. He is developing something called Purity Control. Scully has this substance analyzed and discovers that it contains what appears to be a virus within an ancient kind of bacteria suggesting that the aliens have been around for a very long time. The bacteria contain two previously unknown base pairs that do not occur in nature, which Dr. Carpenter categorizes as extraterrestrial.

Scully suspects Dr. Berube had been cloning the virus within the bacteria and injecting it into something living. She also notes that there is evidence of chloroplasts, an indication that the virus has both animal and plant qualities; this notion is readdressed again in the fifth season opening episode "Redux" and in the use of corn in the movie.

The toxic and acidic green blood also makes its first appearance, although in this case it neither causes the coagulation of the blood nor is it lethal. Mulder is exposed to Dr. Secare and suffers burns around his eyes, nose, and mouth, but shows no signs of the retrovirus infection that he later suffers in the second season episode "End Game." Perhaps the deadly qualities have been bioengineered out of this particular strain for use in humans.

Mulder discovers a laboratory with tanks of hybrids at Zeus Storage on Pandora Street. Both names are significant mythologically speaking. There is not only the obvious connection between the divine nature of the aliens and the primary Greek god Zeus, but also the likely more important connection to the myth of Pandora's Box. Here alien technology represents the contents of Pandora's Box, bringing all manner of terrible things. Like Pandora, man's curiosity is his downfall. However, just like the myth, this box also contains hope, man's one comfort in the face of misfortune. It is this idea that is echoed again in the final scene of the series finale "The Truth."

Deep Throat hints at the Consortium's interest in the x-files when he tells Mulder and Scully that Berube is killed because he is too successful; a clear suggestion that Mulder is initially set up to slow things down. In Dr. Secare, it appears that the Consortium is getting too close to a successful hybrid and Deep Throat uses Mulder to screw things up. The Consortium does not want the terms of the deal between them and the Colonists to be achieved until after the Project has successfully accomplished their super soldier agenda. Unfortunately the DNA transplant takes with Dr. Secare and the first successful hybrid is created. Since the Consortium really only wants the technology, not the end product–they believe that will cause Colonization to begin–Secare has to be destroyed. However, it is later revealed in the sixth season episode "Two Fathers" that Cassandra Spender represents the first successful hybrid as far as the aliens are concerned so there must be some significant difference between Dr. Secare's changed physiology and hers. Like Cassandra Secare does not show any evidence of the presence of the alien sentience; he is not, however, able to heal himself as Cassandra is able to do after her hybridization.

The special abilities he displays; the heightened strength and the ability to breath underwater both of which are characteristics of the super soldiers must be genetic in nature. Since later episodes indicate that the vaccine is not yet viable, Purity must not yet be successfully controlled. The other possibility is that there are two means of viral control that the Project is working towards. The first is to achieve a safe infection where the special abilities are retained but the sentience itself is controlled and the second is a vaccination that will forestall an infection altogether for use in the general populace. The Consortium after all, doesn't want *everyone* to become super soldiers, only the members of their own army.

Deep Throat tells the partners that there are black-op organizations within the bigger one and that one of those groups is responsible for the clean up. There appears to be two main factions within the Consortium. Those members who are using the agreement with the Colonists to gain access to alien DNA and technology for the use in creating the super soldiers and vaccine and those members who want some version of the truth to be exposed. It's likely that it was the first group that assassinates Deep Throat.

Scully asks Deep Throat if Mulder's life is worth the lives of all those who will suffer if the Consortium regains the alien fetus. The idea of the worth of one life is an oft-visited theme on the show. From Samantha to William, the fate of a single life can change the fate of the world.

LITTLE GREEN MEN

"We wanted to believe... we wanted to call out. On August 20th and September 5th 1977, two spacecraft were launched from the Kennedy Space Flight Centre, Florida. They were called Voyager. Each one carries a message. A gold-plated record depicting images, music and sounds of our planet, arranged so that it may be understood if ever intercepted by a technologically mature extraterrestrial civilisation. Thirteen years after its launch, Voyager I passed the orbital plane of Neptune and essentially left the solar system. Within that time there were no further messages sent, nor are any planned. We wanted to listen. On October 12th 1992 NASA initiated the high resolution microwave survey. A decade long search by radio tele-scope scanning ten million frequencies for any transmission by ex-traterrestrial intelligence. Less than one year later first term Sena-tor Richard Brian successfully championed an amendment which terminated the project. I wanted to believe, but the tools had been taken away. The X-Files had been shut down. They closed our eyes... our voices have been silenced.... our ears now deaf to the realms of extreme possibilities."

In the second season opening episode "Little Green Men" it is disclosed that Mulder and Scully are now separated after the events of first season finale "The Erlenmeyer Flask." Mulder is now stuck on wiretap duty–which must be the bottom of the rung for a field agent–and Scully has returned to teaching at Quantico.

Mulder is concerned that he and Scully are being watched and is nervous about meeting with her. Scully on the other hand thinks the powers that be no longer care. She is concerned for Mulder because he seems to have lost his sense of purpose. He is questioning whether his little green men are real or just elves like the one that visited George Hale.

It would seem that Mulder's disillusionment is as troubling to the Walk-Ins as it is to Scully and they try to reinvest him using the equipment at the radio telescope in Arecibo, Puerto Rico. Since the Walk-Ins often communicate obliquely through dreams, it may be important that Mulder has a dream about of Samantha's abduction immediately prior to Senator Matheson's goon showing up. Mulder's dream about the night Samantha is taken is significantly different than the memories he recounts under regression hypnosis; another clue that perception may not be the same as reality.

Senator Matheson–who is apparently Mulder's congressional contact–sends Mulder to the abandoned radio observatory in Arecibo where an anomalous transmission is picked up. He warns Mulder that he only has a short period of time before the Blue Beret U.F.O. Recovery Team show up and that they will use terminal force to stop him. Even though the observatory is abandoned and the power is off, the instruments are all on–another indication that the aliens have some mastery of energy.

Frequently the writers will put hidden clues in non-English dialogue. Once Mulder arrives at the observatory he finds Jorge, a terrified local man hiding in the bathroom. Unfortunately Mulder doesn't understand when Jorge tells Mulder in Spanish that men that aren't really men, find him in the woods and stick him in the bathroom. Jorge then draws Mulder a picture of a Gray. The only possible reason for the Walk-Ins to do this is so that Mulder will find Jorge and hear his story about the aliens.

Mulder is dictating a message to Scully just prior to an encounter taking place. The observatory's tape player records a transmission where a specific piece of Mulder's message is played back–*"Trust No One."* It would appear that the Walk-Ins are not only interested in reinvesting Mulder in his quest, but also in warning him not to believe everything he hears, which is vital to their agenda. Mulder must believe in them, but he can't believe the evil alien lies that the Consortium wants him to believe.

Mulder loses consciousness after seeing a glimpse of an alien form. It is unlikely that anything more happens to him during this time given the aliens' agenda for this particular encounter. The aliens however do make sure that Mulder does not have any hard evidence of their existence by erasing the tape.

In the meantime, Skinner meets with Cigarette-Smoking Man–who talks for the first time– after Mulder fails to show up at his wiretap assignment. They listen to a tape of a conversation Skinner has with Scully where she says she does not know where Mulder is. It's interesting to note that CSM is already confident that Scully will find Mulder–he knows where her loyalty lies.

In "Tooms" the first episode Skinner is in, he is a hard ass and appears to be in CSM's back pocket. In "Little Green Men" there are the first indications that he may not be quite as loyal to CSM as it first appears. A subtle hint is given when CSM runs out of cigarettes and Skinner says he doesn't smoke since smoking appears to be synonymous with evil on *The X-Files*. By the end of the episode it becomes apparent that Skinner isn't in CSM's back pocket at all–although he seems to be stuck dealing with him.

Scully meanwhile has the file that Senator Matheson gives Mulder analyzed and finds out that it looks like the WOW signal–the best available evidence of extraterrestrial intelligence– only better.

BLOOD

While not strictly a mytharc episode, "Blood" plays on a theme that is later echoed in "Wetwired"; a governmental conspiracy to control the populace's perceptions via subliminal messages and fear. In "Blood" the fear aspect is initiated by the use of a pesticide called LSDM that heightens existing phobias which in turn increase adrenaline levels; an increase that causes a hallucinatory state similar to that of LSD; this is similar to the gas seen in "The Unusual Suspects." Given that a hallucinatory state must first be induced and that the messages go unnoticed by others, it is most likely that the victims are experiencing hallucinations controlled by an outside agency in some way. The real point is that the messages come from an external source that requires a specific state of mind in order to work.

Fear is an oft-used mythological catalyst. Myths themselves are frequently stories about how collective or common individual fears are faced and overcome by a recognizable protagonist. *The X-Files* is no exception. The aliens themselves represent a deep-seated fear of the unknown and the various forms of government conspiracy speaks directly to a prevalent distrust of those in power and the things that are suspected to go on behind the general public's back. Mulder succinctly sums up the perpetrators agenda when he tells Scully, *"Fear is the oldest tool of power, if you're distracted by the fear of those around you, it keeps you from seeing the actions of those above."* The same idea sums up the Consortium's need to have Mulder fan the flames of alien hysteria via their use of hoax abductions and encounters. The existence of extraterrestrial beings isn't the real truth they want to keep hidden, it is their own use of alien technology to create various means and methods of controlling the masses, be that through subliminal messages or super soldiers.

SLEEPLESS

In "Sleepless", Alex Krycek, the personification of the hero archetype's shadow appears for the first time. At this point he's an FBI agent, or at the very least is playing the part. He uses the exact same tactics that Diana Fowley later uses in the sixth season (and probably also does in her first association with Mulder) to gain Mulder's cooperation, if not trust. He plies Mulder with subtle flattery and a vocal belief in his ideas. Mulder is particularly vulnerable to this approach, although he seems to be less so when the flatterer is male versus female.

By the end of the episode it becomes apparent that Krycek is really in league with Cigarette-Smoking Man. He gives CSM two vital pieces of information; first that Mulder has found a new contact, and second, that Scully is a much larger problem than they realize, setting up the decision to have her abducted.

Alex Krycek is probably able to beat Mulder to the punch on opening the case because by doing so he allows CSM to accomplish three things; give Mulder a new partner who can use some of Diana Fowley's proven tactics to manipulate him, have the renegade Augustus Cole killed after he inadvertently does CSM's dirty work by getting rid of all the remaining people involved in the original project, and finally to find out if Mulder has found a new contact. Krycek is successful in all three and CSM gets the side benefit of finding out that Scully is still a serious issue that needs to be dealt with.

'X', Mulder's new contact also makes an appearance. All of Mulder's informants play a spirit guide role in the overall myth. Both Mulder and Scully have spirit guides; his are typically human, whereas hers are generally divine in nature. 'X' tells Mulder that Deep Throat died getting him answers and that he doesn't intend to make the same sacrifice– although he ultimately does in the fourth season episode "Herrenvolk."

There were 13 soldiers who volunteer for an experiment while in training for the Marines at Paris Island in 1970. These men have part of their brain stem removed which causes them to no longer require–or even to be able to–sleep. During the Vietnam War they take pills which maintain their serotonin levels. Heightened serotonin levels caused by viewing a tampered with video signal is what later causes the dementia in the third season episode "Wetwired." The lack of sleep also heightens these soldiers' levels of aggression and they indiscriminately kill over 4,000 people during the Vietnam War. 'X' tells Mulder that the sleep eradication project is intended to build a better soldier. Since according to the ninth season opening episode arc "Nothing Important Happened Today I & II" the later super soldiers also don't require sleep either this project is ultimately successful or another option for eradicating the need for sleep is found.

Preacher (Augustus Cole) acts as an avenging archangel exacting vengeance upon the guilty by killing the last remaining people connected to the project. He frequently quotes biblical passages. In the eighth season finale episode arc "Essence" and "Existence" Billy Miles speaks in the same manner as does Absalom in the earlier seventh season episode "Three Words." Preacher uses the ability to manipulate the perceptions of his intended targets to completely fool them into thinking they have actually been shot, burned, or whatever; this ability works on both the original soldiers and on normal people, even Mulder is duped. Since this ability isn't seen in the later super soldiers or alien replicants but is in the WalkIns–like the shaman in the seventh season opening episode "The 6th Extinction" and the blonde in the later "all things"–it must not be a side effect of the experiment. Perhaps Augustus Cole is acting on behalf of the divine and serving justice, much as Scully later does when she shoots Donny Pfaster in "Orison." In addition, Cole is institutionalized for twelve years and psychosis of some kind seems to be a prevalent in those who have a connection with the divine in some form. Duane Barry, Max Fenig and even Mulder in "The 6th Extinction" are notable examples. Scully seems to have escaped this particular quirk even though she seems to have a direct connection to the divine.

Scully teases Mulder that it must be nice to work with a partner who believes his theories. He teases her back about how he's surprised he put up with her for as long as he had. Mulder appears to have realized by this point that Scully's type of partnership is much more effective and desirable than Krycek's or Diana's. He basically tolerates Krycek and no more. Krycek is certainly not immune to the infamous Mulder ditch, but then again, neither is Scully.

DUANE BARRY

In "Duane Barry" Krycek is still operating as Mulder's partner. Mulder seems to have come to accept this although it continues to be Scully that he turns to when he needs help.

Has Duane Barry been previously abducted by aliens or are his perceptions being manipulated, much like the teenagers in the third season episode "Jose Chung's from Outer Space?" If Mulder is telling the truth when he mentions that there is a time discrepancy during the electrical surge at the travel agency; it suggests an alien involvement. He could however, be only trying to gain Duane's trust. It is a critical question–and one that isn't answered–because verifiable time loss appears to be the only thing that the government can't replicate in their abduction hoaxes. Duane's drilled teeth and implants could be caused by the Project's testing since the government has access to alien technology. Since the experience accomplishes nothing beyond helping to cement the reality of Duane's delusions in Mulder's mind, an outcome more in line with the Consortium's desires it is unlikely to be the aliens, but it can not be ruled out. Whoever is responsible for Duane's abductions, be it human or alien, this time they require him to come to a specific location. The same location–Skyland Mountain–is later utilized by an alien ship in the fifth season episode "Patient X.". On *The X-Files* these locations are called light houses which suggest that there is some special kind of quality that the aliens either require or find advantageous in some way. His previous abductions do *not* have this requirement and he is taken from his own home. Since his memories are of Grays versus the human-like Colonists, it appears as though his previous abductions are Consortium ones and his memories are manipulated.

In typical Ten-Thirteen fashion, ambiguity is thrown into the mix with Duane's head injury which could account for his bizarre behavior. Duane generally speaks of himself in the third person, as though he is disconnected in some way to his sense of self; a very Jungian notion, as are many ideas in the mytharc.

There is an interesting parallel in the imagery used during Duane's earlier abduction memories and Leonardo da Vinci's *Vitruvian Man* illustration which is supposed to illustrate the perfect proportions of a man; perhaps a clue as to the desired nature of the super soldiers. The imagery may also echo the crucifixion and subsequent resurrection, a theme later repeated in "Amor Fati."

Duane's implants apparently act as tracking devices, a notion that is first hinted at in "Fallen Angel." Either he uses the implants that Scully has in her possession to track her or do the powers that be send him to her home.

Agent Kazdin mentions the medulla oblongata as the area where a sharpshooter would shoot Duane. It is this part of the brain that controls autonomic functions and relays nerve signals between the brain and spinal cord and is the same area where the pineal gland, which is referenced several times in the narrative, is located. In metaphysical circles, the pineal gland is also considered to be the seat of the soul. If the alien virus takes up residence in this particular spot than that may explain the narrative's logic on how it controls the host and may be yet another clue to the alien as divine. Another interesting note: the medulla oblongata is located in the same area that any organism, alien or hybrid which has green blood, is vulnerable.

Krycek notices in "Sleepless" that there is more going on between Mulder and Scully than CSM realizes–or at least he assumes CSM realizes. Perhaps this is why Scully is abducted in the first place. The Consortium then accomplishes two things; they obtain her genetic material for use in the Project and tamper with her DNA and they give Mulder notice that they test if they can use Mulder's feelings for Scully against him.

ASCENSION

The title of this episode is the first clear identification between Scully and the divine. Here Scully is taken and through her experiences made in a sense divine. With her branched and manipulated DNA she now carries a certain genetic alien-ness; this is the beginning stage of Scully's rebirth into the mythological goddess archetype.

"Ascension" is the first episode where the infamous *"Kill Mulder and you risk turning one man's religion into a crusade."* line is used–this time by Cigarette-Smoking Man. However, since 'X' tells Mulder that Scully's abduction reaches beyond any of them, even Deep Throat it is likely that there is a lot more to it than just a means of dealing with her.

During Scully's ordeal there is a clear psychic connection between her and Mulder. He has flashes of various images relating to what is happening to her. Later Scully has a similar experience during Mulder's eighth season abduction. Perhaps a strong indication of the idea that they are two parts of a single whole.

Mulder is in full Got-To-Find-Scully mode in "Ascension." Scully's cries for help on his message machine are analogous to Samantha's during her abduction. His worse nightmare is happening all over again and he is desperate to stop it.

ONE BREATH

In the episode "One Breath" the character of Scully's sister, Melissa appears for the first time. Mulder–Mr. I'll believe anything–doesn't subscribe to her *"harmonic convergence crap,"* indicating that he's not nearly as open-minded as he likes to believe he is.

Since Mulder sees two helicopters on Skyland Mountain, Scully probably isn't taken by an alien ship at all. In fact, her abduction experience follows more closely those who are taken in a government hoax versus the real deal and there is no mention of lost time. Perhaps she is later taken from the Consortium by the Walk-Ins who return her to Mulder and her destiny. Given Scully's later memories of Dr. Zama and the train cars in "Nisei" and "731," the Project doctors must have Scully for at least part of her abduction. Her chip implant is another clue; it is manufactured in Japan. CSM also considers Scully taken care of at this point, if his agenda is solely to remove her from Mulder's influence (or more likely, remove her influence on Mulder) then he has no reason to later return her. It's more likely that he has nothing to do with her return at all.

If during the time they have Scully the Walk-Ins do something special to her in preparation for her later role as mother of William it could explain the Consortium's interest in a blood sample and Nurse Owen's inability or unwillingness to heal her. To heal Scully may have undone whatever condition the Walk-Ins require. Nurse Owens is the first personification of the Walk-Ins or the divine sent to act as a spirit guide to lead Scully back to life.

Scully has residual protein chains from branched DNA in her blood. The Lone Gunmen theorize that this looks like the cutting edge of genetic engineering and that the technology used on Scully is 50 years ahead of its time. Langly suggests that this branched DNA is a possible byproduct of an attempt at grafting something human onto something inhuman– most likely the work of the Consortium and the Super Soldier Project. Branched DNA also has applications in both virology and in nanotechnology, both later developments on the show.

A vengeful Mulder is initially ready to give up everything to find and punish the guilty parties. 'X' keeps referring to the fact that Mulder doesn't have the heart for what needs to be done–which seems to imply that he can't kill in the name of the quest; however, in the end he doesn't have the heart to become the fully transformed hero. It is important to note that all factions of the Consortium ('X', Deep Throat, Marita, Krycek, CSM and the other Elders) seem to subscribe to the notion that the end justifies the means–whereas when push comes to shove, Mulder and Scully usually do not and when they do it fails. The episode strongly makes this point by showing us a Mulder who is in a situation where he is the most likely to snap and he doesn't do it and Scully recovers. Perhaps this is the outcome that the Walk-Ins are waiting for.

The character of Skinner begins to really develop in "One Breath." For the first time he appears to be solidly on Mulder's side and the story of his death and rebirth in Vietnam it is revealed why. It is yet another instance of a major mythological theme and a suggestion that the Walk-Ins have a hand in his re-covery, perhaps because of his own destiny with regards to the transformation and Mulder's quest.

Scully's vision of her father during her coma is an early indication of what really matters; not the perceived quest, or in this case Scully's father's career in the Navy (both seen in terms of protection of the masses), but the child.

RED MUSEUM

While "Red Museum" is a pseudo-mytharc follow up to "The Erlenmeyer Flask"; the story of vitamin injecting doctors is not where the real mythological clues are. Instead they are hidden in plain sight in the guise of the Red Museum's teachings, which fleshes out the idea of the Walk-Ins and the coming new age.

The Consortium connection–Crew Cut Man–is last seen assassinating Deep Throat in "The Erlenmeyer Flask," and in "The Red Museum" is up to the typical Consortium trick of destroying all evidence of the tests once Mulder and Scully get wind of them. Based on his involvement, it is probably safe to assume that the same Consortium faction–most likely human–that has Deep Throat killed is behind this cover up also.

The experiments being conducted in Delta Glenn, Wisconsin would ap-pear to be part of the super soldier Consortium agenda based on the test results. The kids are becoming increasingly aggressive as they begin changing from their exposure to the injections the doctor has been giving them and to the inoculated beef. They also exhibit signs of perfect health; both would seem to be logical qualities to instill in super soldiers. The substance in the so called vitamin shots and the supposed beef growth hormone is the same as what is found in Purity Control in "The Erlenmeyer Flask." It contains synthetic corti-costeroids which will most likely act to suppress the body's immune system, a vital function if a virus is being administered that the powers that be didn't want the body to be able to fight off. Mulder also suggests–though as Scully points out, without proof–that Purity Control contains alien DNA. If so, that suggests that the injections are yet another attempt at hybridization. Up to "The Red Museum" there have been no signs of alien control via the virus; instead the virus appears to be merely a delivery mechanism for alien DNA that is intended to provide certain benefits such as heightened aggression and perfect health.

Perhaps the hardest thing to put aside when trying to understand *The X-Files'* mytharc is the Judeo/Christian idea of a completely benevolent monotheistic God. The idea of the divine on the show is more accurately identified with the Greek or Roman pantheon of capricious gods and goddesses or the early Judaic Yahweh. *The X-Files* divine duality is typically seen as angels and demons in later Judeo/Christian myths. Here is the first named appearance of the Walk-Ins and their ability to take over during periods of great despair; an idea that is later readdressed in the eighth season episode "Empedocles" with regards to evil. Are these particular Walk-Ins the same as those that rescued Samantha–an event recounted in the seventh season episode "Closure"–or those that instill evil like in "Empedocles" or are they different sides of the same coin? Often times what may appear evil or bad is in fact not. Marie-Louise von Franz cites a story from the Koran in her book *Shadow and Evil in Fairy Tales* that illustrates this point quite well. Khidr is the more accessible aspect of the Godhead, whereas Allah is the transcendent one; in a way like Jesus and God the Father in Christianity.

> *'Khidr meets Moses, who asks him to take him with him on his wanderings. Khidr does not want to do this, for he says Moses cannot live up to his standards and that there will be trouble, but Moses promises to accept everything that Khidr does. At a village Khidr drills a hole in all the fishing boats so that they will all sink, and Moses expostulates. Khidr says that he had told him he would not be able to stand it. and Moses promises again to say nothing. Next they meet a beautiful youth whom Khidr kills, and again Moses complains and is reprimanded. Then Khidr makes the walls of a town fall so that the whole town is exposed, and once more Moses cannot hold his tongue. Khidr then says that they must part, but first explains to Moses what he has done. He sank the boats because he knew that a fleet of robbers intended to attack and steal them and, as it was, the boats could be repaired. The youth was on his way to commit a murder and Khidr prevented his losing his soul by committing such an deed. He let the walls of the town fall because under them there was a hidden treasure which would now be found and which belonged to some poor people. So Moses is obliged to see how badly he has misunderstood and misinterpreted Khidr's ways.'*

This story points out the folly of anyone second guessing the divine, and this includes *The X-Files'* heroes Mulder and Scully.

The Walk-Ins in "Red Museum" are trying to warn the citizens of Delta Glenn about the inherent dangers in the injected beef. The Walk-Ins' contention that those who slaughter the flesh–or basically eat the infected cattle–slaughter their own souls may be a reference to the evils of the Super Soldier Project and/ or the Colonist's colonization agenda. The Walk-Ins want the reuniting of mankind with the divine too, however, unlike the Consortium; their method is one that involves the development of a natural symbiosis between the two resulting in a single organism with one sentience that can be sexually passed this on–in short, William.

A direct reference is also made to immortality, which seems to be a major benefit of the alien DNA. The Walk-Ins also call themselves the second soul in the first body, perhaps a reference to a shared symbiotic relationship; in the Red Museum members it appears to be spiritual in nature, whereas in William it also takes on additional corporeal aspects and a merging of both halves into a single whole.

The Walk-Ins either refer to themselves as The Lord (our first real indication that the divine is alien) or to their lord and master, which may indicate that they are akin to angels instead. They speak of the Dawning of the Age of Aquarius in terms that is echoed almost verbatim by Cassandra Spender in the fifth season episode "Patient X." In metaphysical circles The Age of Aquarius is typically considered to be the beginning of a new age that will be guided by Peace and Love; much like the Mayan notion of the transformation to happen on December 12, 2012. The Walk-Ins make reference to this new age starting in the eighteenth year after the beginning of the new kingdom. It is an interesting number given that the events in "Red Museum" happen in 1994; eighteen years later would be 2012, the designated year for colonization to begin. If Mulder only listens to what the Red Museum members are saying he might have discovered the date he places so much importance on in the series finale "The Truth" many years earlier.

Richard Odin's name may have narrative significance since names usually do in *The X-Files* universe. One big hint is the raven (or crow) that seems to attack the girl in the woods. The Norse god Odin has two ravens that act as his eyes so that he can know what is going on in the world. Odin is the greatest Norse god; a sage and magician who is supposed to return on the final day and vanquish the Power of Darkness.

Finally, another staple of *The X-Files* narrative, the idea of tolerance, is also at play in "Red Museum" with the members of the cult ultimately protecting the children of those who persecute them. The evil doesn't come from those who are different; instead it originates with the much loved town doctor.

COLONY

"I have lived with a fragile faith built on the ether of vague memories from an experience that I can neither prove nor explain. When I

was twelve, my sister was taken from me, taken from our home by a force that I came to believe was extraterrestrial. This belief sustained me, fuelling a quest for truths that were as elusive as the memory itself. To believe as passionately as I did was not without sacrifice, but I always accepted the risks... to my career, my reputation, my relationships ... to life itself.

What happened to me out on the ice has justified every belief. If I should die now, it would be with the certainty that my faith has been righteous. And if, through death larger mysteries are revealed, I will have already learned the answer to the question that has driven me here... that there is intelligent life in the universe other than our own... that they are here among us... and that they have begun to colonise."

"Colony" introduces the mighty morphin' alien bounty hunters who like most of the other aliens are spectacularly bad pilots. The aliens all seem to crash their spaceships fairly frequently; in fact, it appears that crashing is a common method of landing. Perhaps this is an indication that once having fallen from grace the aliens (the Rebels and Colonists) lose some of their control over the ships. In this case the crash attracts the attention of the crew of a fishing boat who then rescue him granting him safe passage to civilization. He calls himself a Russian spy, an interesting identification, especially since as CIA Agent Ambrose; he later characterizes the Gregors as Russian spies to Mulder and Scully. Perhaps these Russian references are intended to play on the American collective fear of the Soviet Union.

"Colony" begins to address the virus in more depth, although in this case in the form of the retrovirus and its accompanying green blood and not the older version that generally uses black oil. In this episode it is revealed that the retrovirus is lethal in humans because it causes an immune response which results in an overproduction of red blood cells and coagulation of the blood. Mulder does *not* have this response in "The Erlenmeyer Flask" when he is exposed to the green blood that Dr. Secare has which suggests that the retrovirus or at least its lethal form is not present in all of the hybrids or aliens. It is interesting to note that when Agent Weiss finds the ABH and the recently dispatched Dr. Baker (a Gregor) he only reacts to the green blood when he shoots the bounty hunter even though the doctor is dissolving at his feet. It appears as though the Colonists are not lethally toxic, yet the Rebels are.

"Colony" also introduces Mulder's separated parents Bill and Teena Mulder–whether they ever actually divorce is never made clear. It's obvious the relationship between Mulder and his father is strained to say the least, although Bill softens up later in the season ending "Anasazi." Either Bill Mulder does not know that Samantha disappears for good when she is fourteen or he is helping perpetuate the lie that the fake Samantha tells, probably to avoid exposing his own involvement.

The events here are the first clear indication that there are different factions of aliens working at cross-purposes. The group that this particular ABH works for (most likely the Rebels) is apparently against the effort to colonize the Earth and he is dispatched to destroy those who are working towards that end. It is interesting that in "Colony" the colonizing aliens are portrayed as the victims whereas the group that apparently holds the power to sanction or not sanction their efforts is portrayed as murderous—a trait that the Rebels display later in "Patient X" and "The Red and the Black." Both the fake Samantha and the alien bounty hunter as Ambrose, tell Mulder and Scully stories that are close approximations to the truth. The main difference is that in the fake Samantha's story they are persecuted visitors only trying to blend in whereas in the ABH's they are spies with nefarious plans.

A main point of this episode is revealed when Scully makes the fateful comment about drawing the line; this comes back to haunt her several times in later episodes as Mulder frequently uses it as an excuse to ditch her and/or to keep information from her. One of the big questions that *The X-Files* myth continually asks is whether the various victimizations caused by Mulder's quest are justified. In illustration, Agent Weiss becomes yet another victim to Mulder's quest. Scully, who is after all Mulder's touchstone, often voices this concern and the answer is central to the spirit of this myth. On the surface Mulder's quest appears righteous, however, the results of his quest would suggest otherwise. Many episodes address this conundrum and generally the ideology that focuses on a single life's (be that human or alien) importance is successful, whereas Mulder's ideology of finding the truth at all costs is not.

Finally, there are two more names with possible enlightening meanings: The name Gregor may be a reference to Gregor Mendel, the Austrian botanist priest whose work gave rise to modern genetics and Ambrose Chapel means "Immortal House of God" suggesting the idea of divinity and the various bodies as possible temples for the colony.

END GAME

Throughout the mytharc narrative there are frequent references to abortion and fertility clinics. Here the Gregors' ties to abortion clinics are necessary to allow them access to fetal tissue an needed ingredient for the Colonist's attempts at hybridization.

In "End Game" it is revealed that the retrovirus will go dormant in a cold enough environment and can be eradicated through enforced hypothermia, transfusions, and courses of antivirals; a cure that is used again in the fifth season episode "Emily" and the eighth season episode "DeadAlive." It appears that both forms of the virus, the sentient older black oil version and green goo retrovirus, will respond to this treatment.

According to the fake Samantha, the colonizing aliens arrive in the 1940s and begin hybridization experiments intended to eradicate their identical natures. The aliens apparently reproduce via cloning and require human DNA to broaden their gene pool which directly contradicts the deal made between the Colonists and the human collaborators to create immune hybrid slaves that Cigarette-Smoking Man later outlines in the sixth season episode "Two Fathers." Neither the Consortium nor the Colonists are sticking to their side of the deal; they are only using it as a smoke-screen to hide their true agendas.

The fake Samantha also tells Mulder that the hybridization experiments are not sanctioned, which implies that the faction that the Gregors represent is not the faction that is in charge whose ideology includes racial purity which sounds suspiciously like the Rebels. Of course, the replicants in season eight also find the results of the hybridization work abominations– William who is born, not artificially created on the other hand is revered.

The captain of the submarine is ordered to torpedo the alien bounty hunter's ship and 'X' later tells Mulder that the alien bounty hunter will not be allowed to leave; a strong indication that this particular one and the Rebels that he represents do not work in conjunction with the Consortium. The alien bounty hunter's ship is apparently able to use a weapon of some sort that renders the submarine inoperable with the exception of battery power; this was purely a defensive move on the ship's part since the sub was preparing to fire a torpedo at it. The alien spacecraft also emitted a constant stream of random radio waves, both possible references to the quantum nature of the divine.

The fake Samantha is unlikely to be an actual clone of the real Samantha; it's more likely that she is the female half of the clones that arrive in the 1940s. They do however know a great deal about Samantha, which suggests that they either have contact with her at some point or are studying Mulder's life. Then again, the ABH knows a great deal about Mulder too, in fact he knows a great deal about how Mulder interacts with Scully and how important Scully is to him. The ABH is not telepathic, however, and must use force to obtain information, a clear distinction between the Grays and the human-like shape-shifters. While the alien sentience may come from a shared original source, the corporeal abilities are apparently not the same.

In the submarine the alien bounty hunter tells Mulder that he could have killed him many times had he wanted to. Since this particular bounty hunter appears to have no problems with murder, he kills the entire crew of the sub, it suggests that there is a specific reason Mulder is left alive, although the ABH does take a pretty big risk leaving an infected Mulder out on the ice. Mulder's interference must play an important role for the Rebels' agenda also.

To a degree; the fake Samantha is doing exactly what Mulder accuses her of, only telling him what she has to. She discloses the basic premise behind the Colonists' plans without really revealing the true breadth of it. As the multiple fake Samanthas later tell him at the clinic; they came to him because they knew he could be manipulated and even though he attempts to walk away, he is ultimately unable to. He does however tell them that he is not their savior, an interesting comment given the messianic nature of the myth and Mulder's personal view of his role as the one. He's right; William is the messianic figure of the myth not Mulder.

The fake Samantha says that the ABH has powers she's never seen before and is unsure about his actual vulnerability to being pierced at the base of his skull. In the fourth season opening episode "Herrenvolk" it's shown that at least some of the alien bounty hunters can in fact survive this maneuver. Maybe the shape-shifters that are specifically designed as bounty hunters are adapted to survive that which would normally kill the viral colony. In the eighth season opening arc episode "Without," Scully does manage to destroy a bounty hunter by shooting it in the neck, so not all of them are created equal.

'X' tells Mulder that he can only win the war if he picks the right battles and that going to the Arctic will not get him any answers. What Mulder does get by going to the Arctic is the faith to keep looking for those answers, although not the wisdom to know how to do it or how to recognize the answers once he has them. If 'X' is playing the mythological role of a guide, he would have realized that Mulder is endangering his real truth by going to the Arctic.

Choice is a big theme in the episode "End Game" and the partnership between Mulder and Scully is affected by two choices in particular. Mulder, in effect, chooses Scully over Samantha on the bridge, regardless of what he hopes the outcome will be or who fake Samantha really is; a definite start to the turning of the tide of Mulder's priorities. Mulder also draws the line for Scully. He makes the choice to leave her behind instead of further risking her life or career because of his personal quest. As it always does, this gets him into significant trouble from which she must extract him; a good example of the basic premises that Mulder and Scully can not succeed without the other and the dangers of making someone else's choice for them.

FEARFUL SYMMETRY

"Fearful Symmetry" is an overlooked and much maligned episode–at least as far as the mytharc is concerned. It doesn't make much sense in the context of the evil aliens, but makes lots of sense if the aliens are divine.

The episode "Fearful Symmetry" is a play on William Blake's poem *The Tyger* which is about the dual nature of God. The way of the divine on *The X-Files* is mysterious and can appear both benign and malevolent, just as the God of *The Tyger* can create something as deadly as the metaphorical tiger, so can the divine of *The X-Files* create something as deadly as man. In "Fearful Symmetry" the aliens are apparently stockpiling animal embryos in an attempt to protect them from an unnatural extinction caused by humankind. Mulder ends the episode asking if mankind's own survival depends on the conservatorship of these same extraterrestrials, which may sum up the aliens' true agenda quite well. Has the divine decided that mankind has forsaken its stewardship of the planet as is suggested in "End Game" or is the divine attempting to preserve humanity through a select and virtuous couple as in the Genesis flood myth of Noah's ark or the parallel Greek myth of Deucalion and Pyrrha (the son of Prometheus and daughter of Pandora respectively)?

"Fearful Symmetry" also highlights the divine's mastery of matter at the quantum level; although here it is imperfect, the animals are returned two miles from the zoo due to an apparent problem with the space-time continuum–or at least that's how Mulder characterizes it. The light–interestingly there is no mention of a UFO–first makes the animal invisible, releases it from its cage (apparently sub-atomically) and finally takes the animal away where it is either artificially inseminated or a resulting embryo harvested.

The animal liberation group WAO's cause appears righteous–freedom– but their actions cause additional deaths; an apt metaphor for Mulder's obsessive quest and its inherent dangers. The zoo with its inhumane conditions and sadistic keeper Ed Meecham is a metaphor for the Consortium and their policies of inhumane experimentation. Willa Ambrose (there's that name again) attempts to straddle the line and balance the zoo's actions against the overzealous actions of the WAO; a probable metaphor for Scully at this point in time.

Sophie tells Mulder that man saves man, a reference to the fact that while the aliens can show the way, only man can make the final choice to follow.

F. EMASCULATA

The episode "F. *emasculata*" is part of the mytharc conspiracy arc and addresses infection by a deadly microbe, in this case parasitical larvae. It also asks–but does not answer–the question of the relative rightness of withholding potentially panic causing information from the public.

Cigarette-Smoking Man has Skinner send Mulder and Scully to the Cumberland State Correctional Facility where a deadly outbreak has occurred. Since the Consortium's use of Mulder hinges on his being seen as a crackpot it becomes apparent by episode end that CSM's agenda is for Mulder to break the story and then be publicly discredited thus minimizing his future effectiveness as a whistle blower. Luckily Mulder's efforts are stopped before doing any substantial harm to his already tarnished reputation.

Scully again tempers Mulder's initial zeal to publicize the truth at all costs. Mulder lives at the extremes, either he wants to tell all–as long as it doesn't involve him personally–or tell nothing. Scully on the other hand attempts to operate within the gray area in between and decides that in this case the truth would cause panic and ultimately more lives would be lost than by the contagion alone. Which approach is the correct one is a question *The X-Files* struggles with through all nine seasons.

The perpetrator, Pinck Pharmaceuticals is the early incarnation of Rousch, the cover corporation for the Consortium and the Project. The head doctor tells

Scully, *"You see what I want you to see,"* a sentiment that could have come from CSM himself.

It is interesting to note the metaphoric similarities between the beetle F. *emasculata* and its deadly parasite and the Grays and the virus. Both act as symbiotic hosts to an organism that becomes lethal when introduced into a human host.

For a pathologist, Scully appears to be extremely cavalier when dealing with a contagion whose method of infection is unknown. Luckily for her Dr. Osbourne shows up in the incinerator room when he does or she would have been the one exposed when the boil burst; another instance of unchecked curiosity causing an unnecessary death. It apparently doesn't occur to Mulder or he's not overly concerned that Scully may be in extreme danger as there is no evidence of Mulder's typical behavior when she's threatened in any way.

SOFT LIGHT

The episode "Soft Light" is a neat twist and marriage of the two basic principals that define the mytharc, science (or what passes for it on the show) and Jungian myth. On *The X-Files*, that which is generally considered to be the realm of science, generally in the form of the quantum world, becomes the domain of the mythic divine. The twist in this episode is that the Jungian idea of the shadow archetype–the dark, negative and generally repressed or unrecognized aspects of our unconscious–is literalized as science in Dr. Banton's deadly shadow. From the mythological standpoint, Dr. Banton's brush with the quanta releases his repressed negative psychological aspects into an actual shadow that annihilates anyone it comes into contact with. Dr. Banton wants the truth to come into him. He gets his wish, although it's not exactly what he has in mind.

Dr. Banton characterizes his shadow as dark matter–theoretical matter that is made up of particles that emit no light and are believed to account for most of the matter in the universe. Dark matter may not be visible, but it does affect other matter by its gravitational force. The idea of the divine works in much the same way, it is invisible and materially unknown, the belief in its existence based entirely upon the effect it is believed to have on the visible world.

The doctor is shown to be consciously a very ethical person, completely distraught over the destruction and death his condition is causing. He has a clear understanding of right and wrong, in contrast his shadow is an indiscriminate destroyer, as he says, *"it'll kill you, it doesn't care who you are."*

One of the reoccurring themes of the mytharc is the deadly consequences of man playing God by attempting to harness and control the divine aspect, whether that's through the manipulation of sub-atomic particles as in "Soft Light" or the more prosaic attempts at genetic manipulation. The real evil on the show is not the aliens, but the men who would abuse their knowledge of the divine as a means of control, whether that's through direct physic manipulation or through the creation of the perfect weapon.

"Soft Light" is the first episode to mention the electric-magnetic force, albeit obliquely. However, the magnetic research origins of Dr. Banton's work would explain 'X's' interest given the aliens vulnerability to magnetite. Here magnetism, or more accurately polarity, is also a metaphor for the idea of positive vs. negative.

ANASAZI

In the episode "Anasazi" it is finally overtly revealed that the infamous they is a consortium made up of International members who have an agreement of some kind. Mulder's father was a member of this group at one time as is Cigarette-Smoking Man. Bill Mulder is afraid that Mulder will find out about his involvement in the UFO conspiracy; something he has successfully kept a secret up to now even going so far as to allow Mulder to believe himself guilty of letting his father down during Samantha's abduction and the death of the fake Samantha in "Colony."

A friend of the Lone Gunmen hacks into the Department of Defense and downloads documents called the MJ files–an acronym for the Majestic 12 documents or the purported government record of the existence of extraterrestrials. The documents are encrypted in Navajo; the same unbreakable code used during World War II. The Consortium is very worried about these files falling into the wrong hands; the question is whose hands are they the most worried about–Mulder's or the aliens'? Obviously they wouldn't want Mulder to obtain and go public with the contents; however, not only is the Consortium withholding vital information from the human populace, but also from their alien collaborators. Presumably these files contain documentation about the vaccine and the Project, both representing information that they can ill afford falling into alien hands as it would give away their double-dealing. Curiously CSM never gives an adequate answer as to why these electronic files are never destroyed.

The word merchandise is used in these files in connection with the abductees and Scully. The use of the term itself in relation to the abductees highlights the fact that the Consortium objectifies them, seeing them as nothing more than chattel to be used in what ever manner they see fit. One of the Consortium's misinformation tricks is to accuse the aliens of seeking that which they themselves are, whereby placing the demonization elsewhere.

Mulder's conversation with his father is intentionally ambiguous. Bill Mulder refers to choices and the repercussions of those choices; an important theme on the show. Mulder must eventually face a similar choice in the ninth season opening episode "Nothing Important Happened Today I" and he, like his father and Samantha, chooses to abandon his child with heartbreaking results. Both Mulder and his father believe themselves to be doing the right thing, when in fact their actions cause far greater harm and the cycle is forced to repeat itself once again. The ninth season episode "Improbable" centers on this notion that the divine may deal you the cards, but it's what you make of them that counts. As is generally the case on the show Bill Mulder is redeemed before Krycek kills him. He lives in a hell of his making and by finally reaching out to his son transcends it.

In yet another play on perception versus reality; Mulder's water is drugged and his ability to recognize reality is compromised with dangerous results. Mulder's obsession is far too valuable to the Consortium for them to merely kill him when he causes problems. Instead as they continue to successfully do, they manipulate his perceptions to meet their needs, this time via a drug administered in his water. Their work requires that Mulder fan the flames of paranoia where aliens are concerned; they want the public afraid, but not in any organized way that could threaten to reveal or jeopardize their plans. However, if Mulder is in danger of getting too close to the truth even he is disposable.

A drugged Mulder is apparently one who has no internal filter. He attacks Skinner for no discernable reason and he accuses Scully of being a little spy. Deep down Mulder still does not fully trust Scully and feels she has an alternative agenda much as a similar fear surfaces for Scully in "Wetwired." Scully must shoot him to keep him from killing Krycek and putting himself in even deeper hot water.

Oddly, the Consortium has a really bad habit of leaving evidence lying around, both electronically as in the MJ files and physically as in the bodies Mulder finds in the buried boxcar. What possible motive could they have had in keeping those bodies, especially given their potential danger in exposing them? The bodies aren't aliens; they are the remains of unsatisfactory hybridization attempts on humans, most likely children given the size of the corpses. They each still carry their smallpox vaccination scar.

7

THE BLESSING WAY

The third season's opening episode is named after the Navajo's The Blessing Way ceremony. According to Navajo mythology The Blessing Way chant is given to them by the Holy People after man's emergence and is sung over someone to ensure good luck and to restore them to an idealized state. On *The X-Files* these Holy People are represented by the Walk-Ins and Albert Hosteen calls them the ancestors. It's important to note that for the Navajo, the Holy People aren't all good, just all powerful, an apt description of the show's aliens.

Samantha's starlight is referenced for the first time in "The Blessing Way." Albert Hosteen refers to this as the Origin Place, possibly a clue about the connection between heaven and the aliens. There is an implication that there is a collective consciousness that is somehow stored somewhere and can be accessed via dreams and hypnosis; it seems to be the glue that binds all souls together. Perhaps Mulder and Scully are connected at this level in some fundamental way and that's the secret of their unique bond which makes sense given the importance of their ultimate destiny together.

While in this Origin Place, Mulder has his first encounters with the dead. Since these visitations always bring with them vital wisdom, it's important to pay close attention to what the dead say. Deep Throat tells him that man's fire and passion is muted or gone after death. He also states that the answer Mulder seeks (presumably where Samantha is) can be found in the void, but not justice–for that he has to continue his journey on Earth. Is he referring to bringing the Consortium to justice? Probably not, since that is ultimately out of Mulder's hands. Instead maybe it is justice for the aliens and mankind by producing the child that frees both from enslavement by bringing harmony and balance back to the world.

In addition Deep Throat tells Mulder to return and fight the monsters within and without; the subconscious and conscious. The biggest monster that Mulder must ultimately face is his obsession and its destructive nature. Until Mulder comes to terms with its control over him, he can never truly achieve transformation.

Bill Mulder makes an appearance too. His comments are just as revealing if seen in retrospect. He tells Mulder that he *"brokered fate with a life to which I gave life."* Basically he tries to do the correct thing by giving Samantha up for the greater good. He now realizes that it doesn't work and he is imploring Mulder to remember that by telling him; *"You are the memory, Fox. It lives in you. If you were to die now, the truth will die. And only the lies survive us."* Unfortunately when the time comes for Mulder to ultimately face his role as father in the one who can influence the next generation, he leaves just as Bill Mulder does before him.

It's interesting to note that when asked his father tells Mulder that his sister isn't there. Based on the events in the seventh season episode "Closure" she has already died at this point so why isn't she wherever Bill Mulder is? It is suggested in "Closure" that the souls that are taken by the Walk-Ins are waiting to be reborn; perhaps they get another chance at life, whereas those who die in the normal fashion don't. If that is the case then Samantha may be in a kind of holding area–for lack of a better term–and is awaiting her new life. Is she perhaps reincarnated in William so that Mulder can have the opportunity to choose differently than Bill Mulder does, whereby correcting the injustice that her soul previously endured at their father's hand? If so, he fails.

His father tells Mulder, *"The thing that would destroy me, the truth I felt you must never learn is the truth you will find if you are to go forward."* Basically, Mulder's dad doesn't want him to face the same moment of truth (the decision) that he does and which destroys him in the end due to his wrong choice. Unfortunately, he realizes that Mulder's destiny is to face the same fate. Since the decision has to be Mulder's to make no one can know how it will turn out until he actually makes it in "Nothing Important Happened Today."

When Mulder asks Albert about where he's been Albert calls it the Origin Place that Mulder carries within. When Mulder asks, *"It wasn't a dream?"* Albert says, *"Yes."* Possibly this is the same phenomenon that Mulder later experiences in the seventh season episode "Amor Fati" with the boy on the beach. Dreams, like the dead, carry powerful messages on the show and play an integral part in obtaining wisdom from the Walk-Ins–if their messages are listened to.

Teena Mulder consistently refuses to give Mulder the answers he seeks even when doing so might free him from the obsession that is slowly destroying him. She's the shadow of the good mother archetype and plays much the same role as Diana Fowley does. She is a betrayer, the antithesis of trust and represents what Scully will become if she fails in her transformation.

Mulder finds the picture of the Consortium members including his father in front of the Strughold Mining Company. He now knows that Bill Mulder was originally part of the Project in some way. On a side note, perhaps the Strughold Mining Company is mining iron ore or magnetite for use against the aliens.

Scully makes a fateful choice in "The Blessing Way" too when she finds the chip and has it removed (whoops). The chip represents both salvation and damnation, she must carry it in order to live, but it comes with a price.

Scully tells her mother that her father would have been ashamed of her. Either she's afraid he would have been angry that she has disobeyed direct orders or it is that she realizes that she should have went with Mulder and not been so concerned about her career. She doesn't do what is right, she does what is correct–there's a big difference between the two in *The X-Files* universe. Doing what is correct usually fails, whereas doing what is right typically doesn't.

Scully undergoes her first regression hypnosis session and remembers that there are men involved in her abduction. In addition, the sounds are all screwed up and there is a siren. Perhaps this is when she is snatched way by the Walk-Ins who ask her if she is all right. She tells Dr. Pomerantz that she needed to trust someone and that she was powerless to resist. Obviously someone rescues her from the Consortium and returns her to Mulder in "One Breath."

Well-Manicured Man warns Scully that she is being targeted. He often acts as a sort of conscience for the Consortium and he truly feels that their work will save the world and ultimately dies for those beliefs in the movie.

There is a difference in Scully's demeanor over Mulder's believed death in "The Blessing Way" versus "This Is Not Happening." While she is definitely not happy about the prospect at the beginning of season three–she is no where near as distraught as she is later in season eight. During this time Mulder appears to Scully in a dream and tells her; *"You were here today, looking for a truth that was taken from you, a truth that was never to be spoken but which now binds us together in dangerous purpose. I have returned from the dead to continue with you... but I fear that this danger is now close at hand... that I may be too late."*

Again, it's very likely that he is referring to their shared destiny and that he fears he is too late to save her from the assassin. Perhaps this is Mulder's subconscious mind speaking to Scully's and while in the Origin Place he knows the truth that they are fated for. It would explain Mulder's comment that she is there during her hypnosis looking for the truth that is taken from her–her destiny, which is wrapped around her ability to have a special child– which binds them together.

Mythologically speaking, "The Blessing Way" is Mulder's first physical rebirth after a brush with the divine. He now stands at the threshold of his destiny and must choose between embracing it or turning away.

PAPER CLIP

The episode "Paper Clip" is all about the sacrifice of innocents in the name of progress and some perceived greater good (Samantha, Melissa, the Jews–even Albert mentions it in relation to the white buffalo). The Project doctors–including Mulder's father–most certainly do subscribe to this ideology and it pervades everything they do and leads only to failure. It is vital to remember this in the context of the grand scheme of things in the mytharc.

Mulder tells Scully that there are truths that aren't on the MJ tape, which is true–their real destiny isn't about exposing the Consortium at all. The MJ tape isn't about love or compassion; instead it details a supreme lack of it.

Mulder tells Scully that it isn't about justice–it's about fate. It's interesting that he also implies that this means a loss of personal choice. He's wrong, the Consortium may never offer a choice, but the divine always does, something that is all too clear when Mulder and Scully are allowed to make choices in the ninth season that ultimately lead to the neutralization of William and his ability to bring harmony back to the world. The divine tries to show Mulder and Scully the true path, but in the end, they must chose which one they will follow.

On the surface, while at Victor Klemper's green house Well-Manicured Man does not tell Mulder and Scully a whole lot about the alien invasion. He does however tell them something extremely important to the real story. He says that Mulder has become his father–in other words, Mulder is going down the wrong road.

Albert Hosteen tells of the birth of the white buffalo calf that signals a great change is coming. It is yet another allusion to William–not so much a direct correlation, but the idea that a child will be born that can change the world. The Lakota believe that White Buffalo Calf Woman brought them the sacred pipe and taught them the proper ceremonies. When she (or what she represents) returns it will be time for the world to be purified and restored to balance and harmony. Perhaps the white buffalo calf dies in "Paper Clip" because Mulder does not fully understand what is told to him during his Blessing Way and continues to chase monsters instead of focusing on the real truth. Mulder wants to take down the Consortium at all costs, when instead he should be creating, not destroying.

Albert Hosteen's belief that Melissa must die so that something else might live is another example of double meaning on *The X-Files*. He may not be talking about one life for another–although that is certainly the case, since she dies in Scully's place–as much as he is referring to the notion that Melissa's death not only allows Scully's continued growth towards her destiny, but also gives birth to Scully's desire for justice, which is another vital role she plays in the mytharc. Then again this idea flies directly in the face of the underlying message that one life should never be sacrificed for a perceived greater good, but perhaps that's the point that the Walk-Ins want to impress on Scully.

Victor Klemper believes that what he did with the Jews is the right thing, it isn't, but that's the point. Just believing your cause to be righteous does *not* make it so, something Mulder must learn if he is to ever truly understand the destructive nature of his quest vs. the creative nature of love.

It is significant that Mulder allows Scully to choose what to do with the digital tape and respects her choice, even though it goes against his own desires. Scully frequently plays the role of Mulder's conscience and voice of reason and he values that. Scully just wants to see her sister; she realizes that all the conspiracy evidence in the world isn't worth losing that opportunity.

The little Grays that Scully sees in the mine are not hybrids like the ones in the boxcar. They are the Walk-Ins who show up to Scully a brief glimpse of proof, but not enough for complete verification (just as the Walk-Ins do for Mulder in "Little Green Men") and to lead them out of the mine to safety.

Even though it is Luis Cardinale who mistakenly shoots Melissa and not Krycek, the Consortium wants to kill him. Apparently Cigarette-Smoking Man wants Krycek out of the picture and uses the botched assassination in an attempt to justify it. Krycek represents an unknown variable, something that CSM in his desire for total control dislikes.

Finally the combination to the mine is Planck 's constant which is the constant h that gives the unvarying ratio of the frequency of radiation to its quanta of energy, another reference to the quantum.

NISEI

The episode "Nisei" introduces the secret railroad and the mysterious boxcars used for the tests on the abductees. The tests are being conducted by Japanese doctors brought, like the Germans, to America after World War II. These doctors are originally part of the Japanese elite unit called 731, which conducts horrifying experiments on prisoners of war. In "Nisei" these same doctors are autopsying what appears to be a Gray but is most likely a hybrid of some kind and are extracting its green blood. Whatever they're doing it's not appreciated by someone else and they are shot.

While trying to find a woman that Mulder believes may be in danger, Scully meets Penny Northern and the other Allentown MUFON women who recognize her as one of them. Like Scully, they too have chips implanted at the base of their necks and like her also, remove them. Scully finds out that Betsy Hagopian is dying of an undiagnosed cancer and that the rest of the women believe they will die the same way, an obvious foreshadowing of Scully's coming battle.

Agent Pendrell attempts to find out what Scully's chip actually does. It appears to be a kind of neural network that operates in much the same manner as memory formation does. Scully theorizes that the chip can know one's every thought placing it in the realm of surveillance; this may be one of its functions, but not its only one.

Mulder is pretty dismissive of Scully's concern over the cancer. As long as she's presently okay he's not too worried; typical Mulder reaction, he tends to live for the moment and not sweat the future.

Skinner is still clearly the alpha male a balance of power that slowly shifts over the seasons. He lets Mulder know that he's taking himself out of the loop on this particular case which causes Mulder to go to Senator Matheson for answers. It's interesting that the senator has a knack for sending Mulder into known dangerous situations where, while he is likely to find answers, he is also just as likely to be killed. The senator tells Mulder that he's stumbled onto *"monsters begetting monsters,"* a reference to the Project's super soldier work.

Chess is used repeatedly as a metaphor for the ongoing struggle between various forces on the show. Senator Matheson tells Mulder that he has to know which pieces to sacrifice and when–another instance of the objectification of human beings.

It's interesting to note that 'X', and later the First Elder, use Scully to communicate with Mulder. By this point in time they have figured out that she has a certain amount of influence over him. Obviously not enough in this case however, since he ignores her warning to not get on the train. The color red and to a lesser degree black, are used frequently and the secret boxcar is being pulled by an engine painted red and black a combination often used to designate the Project and the race between the Colonists and the Consortium to create a perfect hybrid.

731

Scully remembers Dr. Ishimaru from her abduction and the tests that are conducted on her in the bright white place, which turns out to be the boxcars. Her memories of Dr. Ishimaru strongly suggest that she is the victim of one of the hoaxed abductions.

The First Elder tells Scully that the people at the Hansen's Disease Research Facility have been exposed which is why they are destroyed. He is probably talking about the virus, since genetic DNA manipulations alone shouldn't be infectious, of course the reference to a contagion may be merely a smokescreen intended to pacify her. He also tells her why the Japanese scientists are killed–they began doing secret tests that are not sanctioned by the Project; the same reason given for why the Gregors' are killed by the Rebels in "Colony"/"End Game."

Red-Haired Man tells Mulder that the creature on the train is a weapon; yet another early reference to the super soldier program and more evidence that they are man and not alien made. The hybrids are planned to be a standing army that is immune to radioactive, chemical, and biological weapons.

The First Elder tells Scully that he knows everything about her; probably a reference to their choice to use her in the first place. Later in the ninth season episode "Trust_No1" it becomes apparent that she and Mulder have been under constant surveillance for a very long time. The fact that the First Elder helps Scully try to free Mulder from the doomed boxcar and the fact that 'X' rescues him instead of rescuing the alien hybrid suggests that Mulder is still very important to the Project. The First Elder tells Scully quite a bit, although it is veiled in allegorical terms. He sounds horrified by what the Japanese are capable of, which seems particularly odd coming from someone who apparently oversees terrible tests himself; an example of the skewed perceptions of finding one's own work righteous regardless of its nature.

PIPER MARU

The black oil makes its first appearance in the episode "Piper Maru." Since the pilot of the P51 Mustang is still alive fifty years after it went down the black oil can either recreate and reanimate biological material long dead or it enters the plane immediately and puts the pilot into a kind of suspended animation. It can do both based on later evidence so it's a toss up which it uses here. This particular alien colony is apparently from the downed spacecraft first seen in "Nisei" since the French vessel the Piper Maru is in the same vicinity when they discover the black oil.

In "Piper Maru," the aliens' ability to manipulate the quantum world is highlighted yet again in two very obvious ways. First it affects the ability of the French salvage ship to communicate with the diver Gauthier and it is able to create and use very powerful radiation as a weapon and/or defense mechanism at will. Both of these quantum aspects have been shown before in relation to the ships, this is the first time they are directly linked with the black oil too.

Interestingly, the black oil not only protects its host from the radiation but apparently also restores them to perfect health–a nice little side benefit and an indication that the alien sentience does not wish to cause unnecessary harm if it can avoid it. Gauthier is fine after the experience that gives the rest of the crew extreme radiation burns. The effects of the radiation are somatic instead of acute; this means that its effects are limited to the exposed individual's body and not their genetic makeup and is not passed on to subsequent generations. Given the aliens' interest in genetics, this seems to be an important distinction. Apparently a host does not remember what happens during the time he/she is infected and under the black oil's control, or at least Gauthier doesn't which appears to be born out later in the season eight oil rig episode "Vienen." The virus probably switches from Gauthier to his wife because it figures that someone will be looking for Gauthier and it doesn't want the interference. The aliens generally don't kill unless there is no other choice so it makes sense that this alien presence would attempt to avoid a confrontation if at all possible.

In "Nisei" a corporeal Gray is recovered along with the spacecraft; however, the alien sentience remains behind in the black oil. The sentience must then be independent of a Gray's corporeal body or at least can disengage at will. Usually the Grays represent either the Walk-Ins or the oldest version of the virus. Since in the theatrical movie the virus creates a Gray from appropriated biomaterial, it is unlikely that this is the same as the host/parasite relationship it uses with humans. However, the corporeal body is apparently disposable and not fully integrated with the sentience which suggests that it is not necessary for its survival. Since the black oil that Mulder finds on the dive suit and that which is left on Gauthier is free of the sentience (and its tendency to infect a host), it appears that it too is not a fully integrated medium. There is no mention of the virus in "Piper Maru," however, there is a connection between the black oil and the virus in the theatrical movie, so it is likely that the virus carries the sentience and makes use of various mediums and hosts.

The black oil–or more accurately the virus that animates it–has the ability to pick up memories and language from a host. However, it either does not or cannot take on emotions. There is a possibility that the virus is the purely corporeal connection to the divine whereas humans are the spiritual connection. The union of the two would ultimately create the perfect whole. The Mulder/Scully partnership may be a metaphor for this idea of two aspects uniting to become a better whole; the yin/yang principle or Jung's syzygy.

One of the doomed sailors on the submarine makes a comment that has more significance than it may first appear. He says that, *"None of us are going home."* The alien in "Piper Maru"/ "Apocrypha" is really just trying to get home, which to it is the spacecraft that is salvaged in "Nisei." The theme of going home is echoed throughout the mytharc and is also strongly addressed in the "Dreamland" and "Triangle" episodes in season six. That's really all the aliens want to do.

Col. Johanson makes a very insightful comment to Scully that concerns the mythology. He tells her that, *"we bury the dead alive, they haunt us, beg us for meaning. Our conscience is just the voices of the dead trying to save us from our own damnation."* It gives an interesting twist to the dead that visit Mulder in "The Truth."

It appears as though the Consortium–or at least CSM stops the investigation into Melissa's death, no doubt to protect their interests. Scully realizes this when Skinner informs her of the decision. Skinner is threatened and later shot by Luis Cardinale when he doesn't drop the case as he is instructed to do.

The submarine's name incorporates Zeus. There is also Zeus Storage in the first season finale "The Erlenmeyer Flask" and Zeus Genetics in the eighth season episode "Per Manum." All of these things represent the Consortium's Project and probably refers to their attempts to take over the role of the divine.

Contrary to what he probably believes of himself, there is a bit of the chauvinist in Mulder; he assumes that J. Kallencheck is a man and assumes that Jeraldine is a secretary.

Mulder chases Krycek to Hong Kong, on one hand he's looking for the digital tape that was taken from Skinner in "Paper Clip" on the other, he's looking for vengeance, just like Scully is with Luis Cardinale; although they would both prefer to think of it as seeking justice.

APOCRYPHA

The first scene in "Apocrypha" is a flashback to the statement of the last remaining burned Zeus Fabor sailor to a young Bill Mulder and Cigarette-Smoking Man. The theme of the statement is about telling the truth, which the sailor wants to do, but not to the military which he feels sent them on a suicide mission. Of course, he ends up choosing the worst possible people to tell the truth to. He also makes the comment that XO Johanson does the right thing; he sacrifices some so that others might live. A tactic that is consistently shown to *not* work on the show; perhaps this is why Col. Johanson later feels he is damned. Given the episode's title, it's likely that the events recounted are in some way untrue or not accepted as truth; or perhaps it is a reference to the untruths that the Consortium is propagating about the nature of the aliens.

During this episode the alien is trying to find its ship and is willing to trade the digital tape for it. The alien in this episode is unlikely to be a Colonist since they are usually represented by having green blood and not by black oil. In any case, this alien does not appear all that interested in the information on the tape even though it is damning evidence of the Consortium's duplicity. It is using it only as a means of getting home.

Once the black oil takes over Krycek it makes a point of not harming Mulder. It is certainly capable and kills several others when threatened. It doesn't need Mulder to find the digital tape, it has access to Krycek's memories and the key until it gives it to Mulder in the rental car. Since the tape still shows up missing from the locker, either this is a bogus story to begin with or it has some other means of getting the tape; either way, it doesn't need the key. When the assassins' car is run off the road, it even appears to make an attempt to protect Mulder suggesting that the aliens recognize his importance to the overall plan.

The black oil returns to its triangular ship through a spiral design on the top. Spirals are common and powerful mythological symbols usually signifying the journey to find the center–or the divine. In addition ammonite fossils (an organism with a spiral shell) are used to determine magnetic fields. In metaphysical circles, the spiral is considered to mark electro-magnetic energies.

The color red makes more appearances in the "Piper Maru" and "Apocrypha" arc; the red light in Kallencheck's Salvage Hong Kong offices and the door of the room in the silo that holds the UFO. These both represent the use of alien technology by mankind.

In the meantime, Mulder discovers that the black oil itself is really nothing more than what it appears to be–in this case 50 weight diesel oil from either the P-51 Mustang plane or the Zeus Fabor. However, its chemical makeup has been altered by radiation, probably by the quantum nature of the alien sentience. What isn't apparent is if this is a side effect of the weapon it uses or a necessary alteration in order for the oil to be an acceptable medium for the virus.

In an interesting scene change, one of the agents that is helping Scully search for Luis Cardinale says that they've exhausted all avenues except for a sign from God, immediately after that Well-Manicured Man gives Mulder an oblique warning about the danger to Skinner which leads to Scully's capture of Luis Cardinale. Perhaps this is a subtle hint that the divine are aiding Scully find justice for Melissa.

At Melissa's graveside Mulder tells Scully that justice is served, just not in the manner they expect. The idea of justice through the courts of law versus justice through circumstance is readdressed again and again on the show. When given the chance to exact vengeance Scully does the right thing, even though Luis Cardinale is never tried and convicted, justice is served no matter how disguised it might be.

JOSE CHUNG'S FROM OUTER SPACE

The amusing episode "Jose Chung's From Outer Space" illustrates the whole idea of one's perception not necessarily being an accurate representation of reality extremely well. All of the possible interpretations of the aliens are represented in this episode; from the aliens as complete hoaxes to the idea of aliens as the divine.

Jose Chung's writes that rare is the person who finds meaning in another human being. Harold is ultimately focused on love whereas everyone else gets caught up in the whole alien abduction thing. Only Harold maintains clarity, everyone else has muddled and manipulated perceptions of what happens. Perhaps this is a play on the idea that only through love can Mulder and Scully really achieve the real truth, all of their alien chasing consistently yields only muddled and manipulated results.

Jack Schaeffer lays out the whole fake alien abduction thing for Mulder and the Men in Black pretty much explain the Consortium's use for him. The appropriated alien spaceships are intended to be used in wartime as a means of confusing the enemy and the Consortium is using a discredited Mulder to maintain an air of unbelievability around the idea of extraterrestrial visitors.

Does Schaeffer's continued litany of *"This is not happening"* have any significance to the later episode titled the same? Perhaps it is a clue that what appears to be happening in that episode isn't really what's going on. If you combine that notion with the imagery from the ninth season episode "William" that suggests that Jeffrey Spender was held in a chair very similar to the one that Mulder is held in the season eight opening episode arc "Within" and "Without" one has to wonder what really happens to Mulder while he is gone. Jose Chung points out to Scully that words–here through regression hypnosis–carry the powerful ability to transform or create someone's reality.

There are a number of references to popular culture in "Jose Chung's From Outer Space" and it would spoil the fun to list them all here. The two most obvious ones are the imagery invoking *Star Wars* (the bottom of the cherry picker bucket at the beginning) and *Close Encounters of the Third Kind* (Jack Schaeffer's mashed potatoes).

WETWIRED

The episode "Wetwired" acts as a sister episode to the second season's "Blood." Both center on the Consortium\'s use of paranoia inducing drugs and electronics to incite fear with resulting violence. The Lone Gunmen theorize that the cable emitter is inducing a photic-driving response in those exposed to the subliminal patterns. One of the side-effects of an alien 'possession' is epileptic seizures like those Max Fenig suffers from in "Fallen Angel." Inducing the photic-driving response is one of the experimental treatments for seizures and

other neurological disorders; perhaps the paranoia is an undesirable side effect of an experiment meant to reduce this tendency towards seizures. Given this and the reference to serotonin, "Wetwired" would appear to be part of the super soldier arc, since this is where the Consortium's real interest in alien DNA lies.

While Mulder isn't affected by the subliminal pattern because he's red/green color blind, Scully succumbs to it and believes that Mulder is secretly working with their enemies and becomes psychotic. Trust is a central issue in "Wetwired" or more accurately the lack of it. Like the other victims, Scully's paranoia is an overreaction to an already existing fear. Apparently deep down Scully harbors some suspicions concerning Mulder's real agenda and his connection to her; an insecurity that rears its head from time to time throughout the run of the series. Mulder, on the other hand, tells Scully that she's the only one he trusts and while he may actually believe that, the narrative consistently portrays Mulder as more than willing to trust anyone if shown the right carrot. Scully's recognition of this vulnerability in Mulder probably underlies her fear. The narrative also shows that Mulder's willingness in this regard consistently gets him into trouble, just as a lack of trust in Mulder gets Scully in trouble in "Wetwired."

"Wetwired" is also a precursor to the "Talitha Cumi"/"Herrenvolk" arc in that it sets the stage for 'X's' exposure as Mulder's informant and his subsequent assassination. Obviously Cigarette-Smoking Man is trying to smoke out (no pun intended) whoever is relaying information to Mulder. 'X' uses a middle man and then eliminates him in an attempt to cover his own butt.

Another common occurrence in the mytharc is Mulder's tendency to put Scully first when he is forced to choose between her and his quest. On the surface, this behavior may appear to result in the loss of evidence, as it does in "Wetwired"; however, it also is unfailingly the right choice and more often results in his uncovering a bigger truth as in the fake Samanthas in "End Game" and the mother ship in the movie. The one time Mulder puts his quest above Scully by leaving her and William at the beginning of the ninth season it ultimately causes the loss of his son with potentially devastating results.

TALITHA CUMI

"Talitha Cumi" and "Herrenvolk" are both important episodes in understanding Mulder and Scully's real destiny together. It is very important to listen carefully to what is and isn't said and to not make any assumptions—even if Mulder does.

The renegade alien shape-shifting healer Jeremiah Smith is introduced in the episode "Talitha Cumi." Presumably—although no proof is ever shown—he has green blood that the bounty hunters, Kurt Krawfords, Gregors, and fake Samanthas do. It does seem odd that he would stand in front of a gun when he is attempting to disarm Muntz, since unless he carries the non-lethal variant if he is shot he will have kill them all himself that suggests he is from the same strain as the Colonists.

Jeremiah Smith is a hunted man; a bounty hunter is after him—although this one works for Cigarette-Smoking Man and not the Rebels like the one in "Colony"/"End Game." Smith apparently broke some major rules in the rule book by healing someone publicly and CSM wants him taken care of. The bounty hunter is not only dispatched to eliminate Jeremiah, but to also try to smooth the waters in the FBI investigation, which shouldn't be necessary since CSM has so much control within the FBI already. Perhaps it is only Mulder and Scully that the bounty hunter is interested in convincing.

Jeremiah initially works for the Consortium and CSM calls him chattel and a mere clone; suggesting that a clone has somehow less worth than a genetically distinct individual and suggests that he is only a worker drone like those Jeremiah later shows Mulder in "Herrenvolk"; albeit alien in this case instead of human. The Gregors from the second season episodes "Colony" and "End Game" are also clones; however, the Gregors exhibited none of the same abilities so there must be some qualitative difference between the two. Since Jeremiah can morph and heal—just as the bounty hunters do—it's probably safe to assume that his corporeal body at least is similar to theirs. However, like the

Gregors, there are several Jeremiahs who are apparently eliminated leaving only one remaining by the eighth season episode "This is Not Happening."

Jeremiah observes that CSM's whole life centers on fear. He tells CSM that healing isn't the extent of his powers–that he knows everything about him; another ability that the bounty hunters have displayed about specific people, most notably Mulder. He informs CSM that he has lung cancer–knowledge that is probably part of his healing ability. For some reason CSM makes a deal that allows Jeremiah to go free if he heals him. What isn't clear is why CSM makes the deal in the first place when the bounty hunter is shown in "Herrenvolk" to have the same ability. Of course the bounty hunter also requires a good reason for using it and perhaps saving CSM's butt isn't good enough.

Jeremiah also says one of the most important lines in the series when he tells CSM; *"You can't kill their love, which is what makes them who they are, makes them better than us...better than you."* It is this notion of humans and the ability to love that plays a huge part in the discovery of the truth. CSM talks about the inability of mankind to achieve true justice and that as long as their conscience is appeased humans are happy; which again implies that there is a difference between correct (that which appeases humanity's conscience) and right (that which is just).

In "Talitha Cumi" Jeremiah Smith tells CSM that he no longer believes in the greater purpose or the hegemony project that the Consortium is working on. The only solid clue for the answer is held in his name–Jeremiah is probably named after the biblical priest and prophet Jeremiah who breaks away from the Temple and warns the king of a coming judgment and the destruction of Jerusalem due to the Jews use of idols and other sins. He also speaks of a time of restoration and deliverance and of a coming Messiah. Since CSM is the personification of the king archetype and since the prophet Jeremiah is not speaking *against* God, it's likely that Jeremiah Smith is now working against the Consortium's project and not against the Walk-Ins.

Jeremiah obviously knows the importance of Mulder and Scully, or at least is aware of their work since he seeks Scully out and tells her that he has information for Mulder about an elaborate plan, a project, and his sister. It is interesting that Jeremiah makes a distinction between the elaborate plan and The Project, suggesting that he is aware of both the Walk-Ins' plans and the Consortium's. In his archetypal role as prophet, Jeremiah attempts to tell Mulder of both but is stopped from doing so by a bounty hunter.

"Talitha Cumi" offers the first evidence that CSM and Teena Mulder have an affair that produces Mulder. There are several indications throughout the run of the show that CSM has misinterpreted the prophecy and believes that he is the father and Mulder the son referenced in it. Jumping to conclusions seems to be a trait he passes on to Mulder. There is also evidence that suggests that CSM may not be Mulder's biological father at all given that his body rejects Mulder's genetic material in the seventh season episode "Amor Fati." You'd think that he would have run a simple paternity test somewhere along the way, but this too may be further evidence of CSM's fatal hubris, another trait he shares with Mulder.

Teena Mulder for some reason has one of the ice picks used by the bounty hunters as weapons. It seems to be special in some way since in "Talitha Cumi" and "Herrenvolk" it is strongly suggested that these are the only real tools for destroying an alien, however, in the eighth season opening episode arc it's shown that a bullet in the right place will do just as well. For some reason the news of Jeremiah's healing display sends Teena over to the summer house to find the weapon and prompts her to in a stroke-muddled way tell Mulder about it. 'X' either wants the ice pick that Mulder has or he doesn't want Mulder to have access to one. Perhaps as a spirit guide 'X' doesn't want Mulder to mistakenly kill the wrong alien and blow the prophecy.

HERRENVOLK

It is especially important to make no assumptions about anything when listening to the conversations between Mulder and Jeremiah Smith. Pay careful attention to how he answers–or doesn't answer–the questions Mulder asks him; this is a good example of the writers giving clues while misdirecting at the same time.

Jeremiah Smith tells Mulder; *"Hegemony, Mister Mulder, a new origin of species."* in answer to Mulder's question about why the powers that be want Jeremiah dead at all costs. He is probably referring to the Consortium and their agenda of super soldiers and control. Given that it doesn't appear that Jeremiah is working against the Walk-Ins and the messianic child, it's unlikely that he would be targeted by them.

There are at least five Jeremiah Smith clones to begin with and since all but one is ultimately eliminated they must have the same agenda. Perhaps they all represent a single colony or individual alien sentience. If that's the case, then it suggests that each of the sets of duplicates–the Gregors, the fake Samanthas, the Jeremiah Smiths–represents a single alien entity with the same thoughts and agendas. Perhaps this is why they are identical.

The smallpox correlation is brought up again–it is briefly mentioned earlier in "Paper Clip" in relation to the files in the mine. Before rebelling Jeremiah is keeping and maintaining a database of records concerning the S.E.P.–Smallpox Eradication Program. It appears that each person who is inoculated against smallpox has also been tagged in some manner and according to "Paper Clip," a tissue sample taken and stored. The same massive database is referenced again in the eighth season episode "Three Words."

The S.E.P. cataloging seems to be the manner in which the Consortium chooses who is abducted for the tests. They require genetic information in order to pick folks who are best suited for the hybridization attempts. Since at one time everyone is inoculated against smallpox this would be an ideal way to collect this data. 'X' doesn't want Scully to investigate the Smallpox Eradication Program angle, which indicates that it will somehow ultimately work against the Project. At the end of "Herrenvolk" 'X' is assassinated, however, before dying he leaves Mulder a message about where to find his new source; Marita Covarrubias, who tells him that not everything dies.

The use of an unidentified plant and its pollen in the production of the virus is referenced for the first time. Since in the fifth season opening episode "Redux" it is revealed that the alien virus has both plant and animal properties and since in the movie the virus is shown to be manufactured in corn pollen, presumably pollen can also be used to infect hosts–in this case, bees. The bees that sting the repairman appear to pass on smallpox, which suggests that this is the virus and not the alien one that is being manufactured. Given the deadly nature of smallpox, it is likely that it has some special qualities that either the Project's scientists want to include in the super soldier virus or the qualities make it similar enough to the alien virus for testing purposes. Given that in "Zero Sum" the smallpox and bee tests seem to originate with the Consortium, it's likely that this Canadian facility and the clones are connected to the Project and not the Colonists' hybridization plan. Jeremiah Smith and the Samantha clones are both somehow protected from the bees, whereas the alien bounty hunter is not–although he appears to suffer no ill effects from the stings.

The alien bounty hunter in "Talitha Cumi" and "Herrenvolk" is somehow invulnerable to the ice pick weapon, or Mulder misses the crucial spot which doesn't seem likely. It seems to be too deliberate to be a continuity screw-up so it must mean something significant. In "End Game" the fake Samantha tells Mulder that the bounty hunters display abilities that she's never seen before and she isn't sure if they are vulnerable to the puncture at the base of the neck. Perhaps the shape-shifters intended to be bounty hunters have this invulnerability built in, whereas those destined for other work–like those in the eighth season opening arc "Within"/"Without" do not. CSM gets the bounty hunter to heal Teena by reminding him that Mulder is important to the Project which probably refers to his role in discrediting the existence of extraterrestrials.

Somehow Mulder correctly comes to the conclusion that this bounty hunter will not hurt Scully as long as she stays out of his way; this is surprising, especially since the last contact he has with one should have suggested otherwise. In "End Game" the bounty hunter uses Scully to get the fake Samantha – a tactic this one could have also used to get Jeremiah.

What is commonly pointed out as the ultimate Mulder ditch happens in "Herrenvolk." However, in his defense Mulder does not realize that Scully is in any danger when he abandons her because he believes that the bounty hunter is dead. He does later call her to let her know that he is OK–something he does not do in "End Game"–so he has learned a valuable lesson. He is also desperate to save his mother at this point and when someone Mulder loves is in danger he tends to forget everything else.

MUSINGS OF A CIGARETTE-SMOKING MAN

The episode "Musings of a Cigarette-Smoking Man" is supposed to be apocryphal so the specific events, such as CSM's assassinations of Kennedy and Martin Luther King Jr. are not real narrative events so much as they are stark illustrations of CSM's hubris. However, CSM's delusions of grandeur are not the only aspects of his character to be highlighted; probably more important is the peek into his very human and much more mundane desire to be a writer of pulp detective stories.

CSM's apparent power to decide even who wins the Super Bowl is a reference to his identification with the king archetype which is apparently crown that he doesn't always want to wear. "Musings of a Cigarette-Smoking Man" is a sister episode of sorts to the seventh season's "En Ami," deep down CSM doesn't want to be the monster or destroyer and truly believes himself to be the one trying to save the world. In this episode CSM destroys the force of change– in the form of Kennedy and Martin Luther King–in a mistaken belief that he is preserving a way of life that should remain the same—the denial of the transformation. Like Mulder he is mistaking the divine for a fearsome force that must be put down and also like Mulder, it is this inability to truly understand the true transforming nature of the aliens that makes him ultimately a destroyer instead of a creator.

"Musings of a Cigarette-Smoking Man" also deals with the idea that a fairly insignificant and seemingly unrelated event–seen here as the various rejections of CSM's manuscripts– can have far reaching and potentially disastrous results. If CSM is able to sell his detective stories he will resign his power and many future horrible events could be avoided. Without CSM's influence Mulder may be better able to maintain his early wonder about the aliens and not fall victim to the evil alien story that fuels his quest and ultimately keeps him from achieving his true destiny; this is an echo of the prophecy's notion that the father's influence decides the son's chosen path and another reminder that sometimes doing the less glorifying thing is the best choice.

TUNGUSKA

In "Tunguska" it is revealed that at least one colony of viral aliens came to Earth in 1908 in a meteor that originated from Mars, probably eons ago. The virus can apparently survive extremely long periods of time since the black oil that is found in the rock is still active and has presumably been trapped there for four billion years.

The fourth season episodes "Tunguska" and "Terma" are vital ones for Mulder's side of the equation. It is in these episodes that with his infection by the black oil Mulder takes on the alien or divine nature that plays such a pivotal role in the creation of William. The vaccine only temporarily disables the virus; it does not destroy it; an important distinction that comes back into play in the sixth season finale "Biogenesis" and Mulder's reaction to the rubbing taken from the ship in The Ivory Coast.

Well-Manicured Man is extremely worried about Mulder going to Russia. While WMM often acts in the best interest of the Walk-Ins, it is most likely unwittingly. He believes, as does CSM that the virus is a destructive force that must be stopped or their power stolen. Unlike CSM, however, he has no personal agenda when it comes to Mulder and only wants what is beneficial to the Project. There may also be some connection to the prophecy that is not immediately apparent. If WMM is familiar with the prophecy and believes, as CSM apparently does, that Mulder is the messianic figure recounted in it, then he may be concerned that Mulder remain unexposed to any alien influence that could alter his allegiance to mankind.

In his behavior with Krycek, an important side of Mulder is also revealed and later echoed in "Paper Hearts"–his inherent violence and desire for vengeance; the fuel that drives his quest and which may ultimately underlie his transformation into a destroyer instead of a creator. As the personification of Mulder's shadow, Krycek's twin desire for wrecking vengeance on Cigarette-Smoking Man is an illustration of just how much Mulder is ruled by his darker nature underneath the G-Man trappings. Krycek also tells Mulder and Scully that he wants to expose CSM (and presumably the Project), yet another ruling aspect of Mulder that ultimately comes to no end. Mulder can't affect any kind of positive transformation in this manner, which is illustrated in this early episode by its affiliation with the desires of the shadow.

In "The Blessing Way" Scully comes to the realization that doing what is right (just) is not necessarily the same as doing what is correct (legal). She doesn't make the same mistake in "Tunguska" that she does in "Anasazi"; which is to worry about the legality in place of the morality. Scully comment at the beginning of "Tunguska"; *"I left behind a career in medicine to become an FBI agent four years ago because I believed in this country. Because I wanted to uphold its laws, to punish the guilty and to protect the innocent. I still believe in this country. But I believe that there are powerful men in the government who do not."* illustrates her role as justice as counterpoint to Mulder's truth.

Scully again tells Mulder that she doesn't know how far she can follow him and he again ditches her. He seems to do this only when he feels it would be unfair to expose her to danger or career suicide for his own agenda and as it usually does, it gets him into trouble.

TERMA

In the episode "Terma" it is revealed that tests are being performed on the elderly at nursing homes in which they are being infected with the virus via the black oil. One woman is in a lot of pain from unrelated health issues and the virus dies when she does. The virus doesn't attempt to heal her, which probably means that it can't for some reason. The virus that the scientist is infected with has only slightly thickened his blood. The effect appears to be a much milder form of the reaction to the retrovirus in the green blood–perhaps evidence that they are basically the same–just different mutations. The earlier less evolved version also appears to lack the special abilities and perhaps even the higher sentience of the virus seen in earlier episodes. Perhaps the retrovirus is a mutation that developed in order to facilitate a successful symbiotic though not fully transformed relationship with the shape-shifters and their green blood. The early form of the virus found in the rock however, may not require this mutation and is consequently much less lethal to humans, thus being a much more desired strain for those attempting to create a super soldier or for the Walk-Ins attempting to create a perfect alien/human merging. The comments that the prisoner makes to Mulder about the persistence of life applies to the virus also. It isn't evil at all; it's just trying to survive. The real evil is in what the Consortium is trying to achieve by using it.

The question not answered in this episode is whether Dr. Charne-Sayre, the virologist working on the vaccine for the US, is working on a vaccine to ultimately protect the general populace in which the virus is either completely destroyed or deactivated with no residual special abilities or in the super soldier program or both. Krycek has Pescow kill Dr. Charne-Sayre in yet another example of the shadow using violence in its attempt to transform. It's interesting to note that by doing so he also kills the love between WMM and the doctor.

CSM knows that Mulder is in the Russian gulag and that he has subsequently escaped. He doesn't learn this from Krycek; not only because Krycek hates him, but because Krycek is taken by Mulder during his escape and has no opportunity to contact CSM and is probably another indication that CSM has his fingers in all the pies or as the king has a certain amount of omniscience.

The episode "Tunguska" reveals for the first time that the virus colony attaches itself to the pineal gland of the host. In parapsychological circles the pineal gland is significant in the appearance of psychic phenomenon which may explain how the virus accesses and activates latent telepathic ability. Interestingly enough the location of the pineal gland also corresponds to the believed location of the chakras; a probable illustration of the connection between the aliens and the power of emotions–most importantly love as seen in the seventh season episode "all things"–to affect transformations.

Pescow takes the Mars rock all the way to Canada and puts it into a specific oil field and then blows up access to the well effectively placing the oil out of reach. Perhaps this is an attempt to return the less mutated original form of the virus to its home in the earth.

NEVER AGAIN

Throughout the narrative Mulder displays consistent character traits of an autocratic nature and an apparent inability to realize that Scully is as fully invested in the x-files as he is; a tendency he never out grows and is clearly apparent even in "The Truth." Scully's lack of a desk is the symbol that the writers use to illustrate this. Of course Scully can get her own desk; however, that's not the real point. The desk is an important symbol of Mulder's inability to give her equal status something only he can give her because it is a change in *his* perception that she requires and not her own which is highlighted later in "Patience" when she gives Doggett his own desk and comments about how she never had one. She is offering Doggett the respect as an equal that she feels she never receives from Mulder. In "Never Again" it is this need for Mulder's approval that she's rebelling against.

As Scully tells Ed Jerse, she has a thing for daddy figures something that becomes even more apparent in her relationship with Daniel Waterston in "all things." While Mulder is more subtle about it than Daniel is, he does treat her like a subservient and she finally rebels as she is apt to do. The interesting thing is that this time she doesn't leave as she once does with Daniel.

Even though she denies it, her feelings in "Never Again" *are* about Mulder, or at least the catalyst for them is. However, her choices in the episode are all about her. The tattoo symbolizes the unbreakable cycle of Scully's life and her need for approval. It must be very hard to give everything that she has for the x-files and still not earn more than a *"you were just assigned"* from Mulder. Later in "One Son" he even tells her not make it personal. Here is a side of Mulder on display that normally keeps him emotionally isolated. Scully's behavior, on the other hand, illustrates what causes her to be overly stoic and emotionally closed off. The same concepts are played for laughs later in "Bad Blood" and more seriously in "Milagro."

In "Milagro" Phillip Padgett says that motive is always the hardest aspect to get a handle on; that seems to be the central theme of the episode. In the end he does finally understand Scully's motivation–she wants to get Mulder's attention, which she apparently feels she doesn't have at this point in the narrative. Add to this the events in "Never Again" and Lyda's assertion that Scully is codependent in "How the Ghosts Stole Christmas" and a clear picture of Scully's driving force becomes apparent.

In both cases, Jerse and Padgett choose to save Scully by destroying their obsessions in the furnace. In doing so, they are healed. Jerse is saved from his own inner demons and in death Padgett becomes a creator instead of a destroyer and is redeemed. In order for Mulder to not follow in his father's destructive footsteps he has to symbolically sacrifice his obsession with his personal quest (symbolized by Padgett's manuscript and Jerse's tattoo). Padgett may die, but he literally and figuratively gives his heart in doing so which is something Mulder never completely does. The Lone Gunmen try to convey this to him in "The Truth" by telling him to pursue perfect happiness and never look back. Of course, he doesn't listen.

In other words, Mulder can't have his cake and eat it too; *something* has to be thrown into the furnace. Jerse and Padgett may destroy their obsessions and in a way a part of themselves, but they are also both released from its destructive control. Scully stands as the one who is able to break through and mean more to both of them, which allows them to find peace.

MEMENTO MORI

"For the first time, I feel time like a heart beat. The seconds pumping in my breast like a reckoning. The numerous mysteries, that once seemed so distant and unreal, threatening clarity in the presence of a truth entertained not in youth, but only in its passage. I feel these words as if their meaning were weight lifted from me knowing that you will read them and share my burden as I have come to trust no other. That you should know my heart, look into it, finding there the memory and experience that belong to you, that are you, is a comfort to me now as I feel the tethers loose and the prospects darken for the continuance of a journey that began not so long ago. And which began again with a faith shaken and strengthened by your convictions. If not for which I might never have been so strong now as I cross to face you and look at you, incomplete, hoping that you will forgive me for not making the rest of the journey with you."

According to the Webster dictionary, memento mori means either a reminder of mortality or a reminder of man's failures or mistakes; both apt descriptions of the events in this episode. Here Scully is diagnosed with a nasopharyngeal tumor caused by whatever is done to her during her abduction: a stark reminder of her own mortality and a result of the Consortium's failures. The nature and location of the tumor makes it extremely difficult to treat and it is the same kind of cancer that has been systematically killing off the women from the Allentown MUFON chapter that Scully meets in the third season episode "Nisei."

The Kurt Krawford hybrids are introduced in "Memento Mori" and like the other corporeal human-like aliens have to be killed by a puncture to the base of the neck– preferably with one of the special ice picks. Once dead they dissolve into the green goo. Based on the lack of any negative effect on what appears to be a human assassin, the Kurts must be non-toxic. The Kurts call the MUFON women their mothers by which they mean that their human DNA comes from that which is contained in the ova harvested from the female abductees. The procedure that is used to do the harvesting of ova leaves the female abductees infertile and prone to cancer. Both Penny Northern and Betsy

Hagopian had been treated for this infertility at The Center for Reproductive Medicine, in Lehigh Furnace, Pennsylvania, which may involve the same super soldier embryo work that is referenced again in the fifth season episodes "Christmas Carol" and "Emily" and in the eighth season episode "Per Manum." The Kurts say that they are among the end results of the work that produces the hybrids in the tanks that are initially seen in the first season finale "The Erlenmeyer Flask." They are the products of the Consortium and are illicitly sabotaging the Project in an attempt to save the MUFON women.

Like the Jeremiah Smiths all of the Kurts seem to know what any of the others do. The second Kurt that Mulder meets at the Lombard Research Facility is indistinguishable as far as his behavior and knowledge of Mulder from the one that is killed at Betsy Hagopian's house. They appear to function in the same colony-like way that Jeremiah does. They aren't the bad guys at all; they are just as disgusted with what the Consortium is up to as Mulder and Scully and are actively working to subvert it. In this context, the aliens have been enslaved via their DNA.

One of the Kurt Krawfords is downloading a file directory from Betsy Hagopian's home computer that references files stored at The Lombard Research Facility. Scully's name shows up in this file directory and the file itself contains information about the gene code sequence that is found in her blood post-abduction in "One Breath." Since in mythological terms the presence of alien DNA establishes a certain kind of divinity, it appears that Scully has been prepped to take on her later divine nature as the goddess archetype.

It is interesting in retrospect to note that cancer basically acts and kills the same way that the alien virus usually does. In Chris Carter's typical voice-over fashion Scully says; *"This is the evil of cancer, that it starts as an invader, but soon becomes one with the invaded, forcing you to destroy it but only at the risk of destroying yourself."* Cancer is the body's reaction to some stimulus that causes cells to mutate and grow out of control. Perhaps this is a literal and metaphorical reference to the alien virus and the reaction it inspires. On one hand, the virus acts as a catalyst and it is deadly because it causes an overreaction that either causes an immune response that congeals the blood or an over stimulation of the pineal gland that causes severe mental illness and/or catatonia. On the other, metaphorically speaking, the aliens themselves aren't consciously destructive; it is the unavoidable human reaction that their nature inspires that is.

Penny Northern's comment to Scully that they had let her come to Scully during the procedures and that she didn't know why since human compassion isn't something they have appears on the surface to refer to the aliens. However, based on "Nisei" and "731," it would appear that it is the Consortium that abducts these women and conducts the tests suggesting that it is the Project's human doctors and scientists who lack compassion, not the aliens.

Since the assassin is pretty persistent in his attempts to kill Mulder at the Lombard Research Facility, he must have something that Consortium feels is more important to them than he is. He really hasn't seen anything he doesn't already know or at least have strong suspicions of so it must be the vial of Scully's ova that he steals. If Scully is rescued by the Walk-Ins during her abduction the Consortium may realize that she is special in some way and want to maintain total control over her ability to reproduce or hoard her ova for their own use. After all the prophecy does state that there will be a special child born to a barren mother and given the Walk-Ins interest it's reasonable to assume that she may be the one.

Mulder tells Scully that the truth will save her; that it will save both of them. Since the truth is ultimately the transformative power of love that produces the messianic child, this comment means a great deal in the overall myth.

TEMPUS FUGIT

The episodes "Tempus Fugit" and "Max" explore two of the central themes of the mytharc; the idea that it is the government that is the real evil and the idea that, as Scully says, *"no one gets there alone."*

Since the plane loses 9 minutes at some point before going down the real aliens are involved in some fashion. In fact, it is later suggested that the nine minutes are lost while the aliens have the plane out of time in an attempt to recover the stolen technology without doing any harm. Here again the aliens go out of their way to not kill the innocent. In contrast, poor Pendrell is killed, another victim of Mulder's quest and as is usually the case with regards to sacrifice on *The X-Files;* his death is ultimately in vain, Louis Frish is still taken by those in power.

Louis Frish tells Mulder and Scully that a military aircraft shoots down Flight 549, another instance of the government using the apology of one crime to hide the existence of a far larger one. The same apology as policy theme is explored in the third season episode arc "Piper Maru"/"Apocrypha."

In yet another reference to the quantum nature of the aliens and their technology, whatever Max Fenig is carrying emits a great deal of radiation–enough to burn him and the passenger sitting next to him. Apparently whatever this thing is, the Walk-Ins really want it back. Since this particular faction of the aliens are generally shown trying to fix things that either their own renegades (the Rebels or Colonists) or man have screwed up, this thing when put back together and fully operational may be a weapon of some kind, or have weaponry applications; especially given that it was previously in the hands of a defense contractor.

There is a second spacecraft–presumably the same one that later abducts Sharon Grafia– searching for the wreckage of the downed UFO in the lake. Mulder finds this UFO and at least one Gray who may or may not be dead given that these guys can live in a sort of suspended animation and under water. Also, as seen in "Piper Maru" and "Apocrypha" the alien sentience can disengage from the corporeal body if another suitable medium or host is present.

The Walk-Ins abduct and then drop Sharon off at flight 549's crash site perhaps trying to get the investigator to refocus his attention back there and find the real truth about what happened. Sharon's abduction doesn't do much more than that since she doesn't have any of the technology.

Mulder actually remembers Scully's birthday for the first time and gives her the Apollo 11 key chain which symbolizes their partnership and the idea that no greatness is ever achieved solely by one individual. Here is the crux of Mulder's transformation; he cannot find true completion until he moves beyond his self-obsession as the one.

MAX

Scully has a nosebleed immediately following Pendrell's death. Scully's nosebleeds seem to happen whenever she is actively investigating something that involves the divine and/or their interest in her in some way. She has one when she and Mulder first find the Kurt Krawfords in the episode "Memento Mori," during their investigation into the ghosts in "Elegy," and later during the FBI panel in "Redux"–that one being the granddaddy of them all.

Based on the flashback, the aliens do not intend for Flight 549 to crash and if the military aircraft never intercepts it, the plane would have safely landed with no one the wiser–except that whatever Max is carrying would be gone. The passengers of Flight 549 are victims of the government and their greed for alien technology and not of the aliens themselves.

Through the aliens' ability to manipulate matter at the quantum level, the alien ship is able to protect the plane during the nine minutes the door is off–it isn't until the military plane shoots the UFO down that Flight 549 reacts to the loss of air pressure and crashes. If the aliens have this kind of technology why can't (or won't) they protect themselves from fighter planes? Based on the defensive actions taken against the Zeus Faber submarine by the spaceship in the second season "Colony"/"End Game" episode arc, they can successfully defend themselves if they want to so it's more likely that they sometimes choose to not do so although given the number of lives lost, it's unclear why they would choose to forgo defending themselves and the plane in this particular case. Perhaps this is about choice and the Walk-Ins refusal to make it for others.

"Max" really deals with the idea of innocents dying not only because of the Consortium cover-up, but also because of the attempt to reveal it. All those folks on Flight 549, Pendrell, and the military air-traffic controller die needlessly. Scully wants to know what it is that they are all dying for–the lies or the truth. Mulder says it has to be for the truth–or at least his version of it–as though that justifies it. Mulder also tells Scully that if they don't find out who kills Max and Pendrell that their lives will have no meaning–yet another Mulder fallacy and what he has yet to learn; the victims' lives already have meaning because someone cares for them.

Who is the agent in charge that Scully says she has to talk to? In the past she and Mulder have always reported directly to Skinner, yet in "Max" he doesn't know about the federal marshals that Scully calls in. Obviously whomever it is that she contacts lets the cat out of the bag and Garrett knows where to find them. Why does Garrett try to shoot Louis in the first place? The order for the federal marshal protective custody has already been countermanded and the military is going to arrest Louis anyway. The only explanation that makes sense is that there are four different agendas at work in this episode arc; the aliens', Mulder and Scully's, Garrett's and whomever he works for, and the military's.

The assassin Garrett tells Mulder on the plane; *"Look out your window, Agent Mulder. You see the lights? Now, imagine if one of those lights flickered off. You'd hardly notice, would you? A dozen... two dozen lights extinguished. Is it worth sacrificing the future, the lives of millions, to keep a few lights on?"* It's important to remember that Garrett is the bad guy. His philosophy sounds good on the surface–but it is the same rhetoric the Consortium spouts all the time so it is unlikely to be the right one in the end. It is this ideology that is the underlying cause of the strife in *The X-Files* universe. Unless decisions are based on recognizing the value of each and every individual, no resolution (balance and justice) can be achieved. When the right choice is made, no one dies and no sacrifices are required.

Why do the aliens end up taking Garrett? He isn't an alien–he is distinctly human since he bleeds red blood when he is shot (this proof is probably the narrative reason he is shot to begin with) and he spouts the same sacrifice the few for the many false ideology of the Consortium. Perhaps this is an attempt to illustrate that justice is ultimately served by the divine; as is typically the case they have things under control without Mulder's intervention.

One important final note here is that Max Fenig knows before getting on the plane that he is putting innocent lives in danger, but does so anyway and they all subsequently die. In other words, he doesn't do the right thing regardless of how correct it may appear to be. Every time someone (Mulder and Scully included) put finding some proof or personal version of the truth above human life it backfires and an innocent is either hurt or killed and it happens consistently in both the mytharc and monster of the week episodes.

ZERO SUM

The episode "Zero Sum" acts as a sort of allegory highlighting the inherent problem with Mulder's quest. Here Skinner believes that he's doing the right thing and perpetuates a bigger evil trying to achieve it. What's important is that Skinner's sacrifice in offering himself up doesn't work and Scully still has cancer. Like Skinner in "Zero Sum," ultimately Mulder's inability to come down off of his self-imposed cross causes his failure too. Skinner in his various subterfuges even uses some of Mulder's tactics. Skinner's actions in "Zero Sum" only act to place him even further under Cigarette-Smoking Man's thumb, just as Mulder's actions generally only act to further the Consortium's agenda instead of hindering it.

"Zero Sum" readdresses the bee angle that is first introduced in the season opener "Herrenvolk"–and continuity with the reference Dr. Valedespino makes to Skinner about Mulder's killer bee call six months earlier. Here someone is using the US Postal Service to mail very aggressive bees infected with a strain of smallpox; an apparently risky proposition unless the bees escape is the intended result. The whole operation is probably a test scenario for the effectiveness of the bees as a vector for a virus. The same program is referenced again in the theatrical movie. The However, the Consortium Elders see the event as a breach which suggests that they aren't directly behind it, although it is likely that CSM is.

The postal worker who is killed by the bees suffers from a mild form of anemia; a condition that comes up again in the season five episode arc "Christmas Carol"/"Emily" as a problem the virus has a particularly hard time dealing with.

Someone is with Marita when she calls CSM at the end of the episode. It can't be Skinner because he has just left CSM after threatening him. It is most likely Krycek, foreshadowing the affiliation later shown in the fifth season episode "Patient X" and setting Marita up as a triple agent working for and against CSM, Krycek and Mulder whenever it best suits her purposes.

DEMONS

The episode "Demons" Mulder allows holes are drilled into his frontal lobe which is the location of the so-called God Module the area of the brain theorized to be control man's conception of the divine. The same area is later associated with Gibson Praise and his telepathic abilities.

"Demons" calls into serious question Mulder's recollections of the night Samantha is taken. According to this episode there are no aliens involved at all, just Bill, Teena and Cigarette-Smoking Man. Of course this may not be the actual night in question, but it's apparent that there is some conflict involving Samantha between Mulder's parents and CSM. In "Demons" Mulder is now at an emotional stage where he will apparently try anything to regain his memories of that fateful night; perhaps his suspicions that Scully's illness is somehow connected to her own abduction and his fear over her impending death is fueling his sudden desperation.

From Mulder's flashbacks it's apparent that Teena Mulder is upset at the idea (not surprisingly) of Samantha being taken and that Bill Mulder is trying to tell her that the orders came down from somewhere–presumably the Consortium. Here Bill puts his duty above his family and pays the price just as Mulder does later in the ninth season with the loss of his son William. William may not become the lab rat that Samantha does, but his ability to transform the world is seriously compromised.

The abductees who undergo Dr. Goldstein's treatment to recover buried memories are all systematically committing suicide and exhibit episodes of repetitive behavior before hand; a symptom originally seen in the first season episode "Deep Throat." The suicidal behavior must be connected to the treatment and not to the previous abductions since Mulder becomes suicidal too and up to this point he had never been taken–at least that he knows of. Of course he is infected with a latent form of the virus from his escapade in the Tunguska gulag from earlier in the season so there is a possibility that the behavior is associated with the virus and not with the treatment itself. However, given the episode's theme of unethical medical practices, the treatment is more likely to be the catalyst than the aliens.

Scully certainly trusts that Mulder won't physically hurt her no matter what–and he doesn't. She echoes the same thought again in the seventh season opening episode "The 6th Extinction" when he is experiencing another psychological breakdown. No matter how disconnected from reality Mulder is, he maintains his connection to Scully. She is however, very concerned about the lengths that he'll go to in order to remember what happened to Samantha and the events in "Demons" illustrates that perhaps this obsession is not a healthy or righteous one and better let go of before it destroys him.

On an interesting side note; names are reused a lot in *The X-Files* universe. In "Demons" the name Cassandra shows up for the first time with David and Amy.

GETHSEMANE

In the episode "Gethsemane" Michael Kritschgau–an employee for The Pentagon Research Division–draws Scully's attention by stealing the ice core sample. He then tells Mulder and Scully that they are being manipulated and have been all along. They are being led down very specific paths. He also tells them that the whole alien thing is a big hoax perpetuated to hide the real work. Mulder is being used to give a sort of credence to it. While not entirely accurate about the existence of aliens; his point about the Consortium using Mulder is right on the money.

"Gethsemane" is Mulder's version of the agony in the garden. It's important to look at what cup he wants taken away; it is not his quest, he's hanging onto it tooth and nail to the point of ignoring the very real impending death of Scully. What he doesn't want to face is the fact that his refusal to acknowledge the vulnerability to manipulation that his single-mindedness allows is what causes Scully's cancer in the first place; it is this realization that takes him to the brink of suicide and the abandonment of his real destiny. That's not to say Mulder's isn't supposed to be an agent for the truth; however, it's neither the truth he believes in nor is the path he runs headlong down the one that will lead to it.

The ice core sample taken from around the frozen Gray has genetic material within it that Dr. Vitagliano characterizes as a chimera; which, as is typical on *The X-Files*, has a double meaning. Kritschgau tells Mulder and Scully that this biomaterial is used by the Consortium to build the body that Dr. Arlinsky finds. The Gray that Arlinsky autopsies does not have green blood. Since the one in the third season episode "Nisei" did, either this is an oversight or an intentional clue that the Gray in "Nisei" is not exactly the same thing as the Walk-Ins. It is probably a failed hybrid for the super soldier program. Instead this Gray is a clone of the bodies used by the original strain and the Walk-Ins.

Babcock kills everyone and then shoots himself in order to avoid suspicion. He then buries the alien body until Arlinsky returns with Mulder. Since he is eventually killed by the same assassin that shoots Arlinsky he is probably a plant designed to draw Mulder's waning attention back to the alien threat.

According to *The X-Files'* narrative, there really are aliens so while Kritschgau is apparently sincere in his attempts to enlighten Mulder and Scully like everyone else he knows only part of the truth. What he does know is that Mulder is being set up to further the Consortium's agenda which is primarily the creation of the super soldiers. What he doesn't know is that there really are aliens and that this is where the advanced technology is coming from.

Scully tells Father McCue that it isn't like her to go running back to the church just because she's ill–that it would be lying to herself and to him. In fact, at this point in the game she sounds more agnostic than anything. Especially when she tells Mulder that she doesn't think much about whether the belief in God is a lie and that she doesn't believe it can be proven either way. Scully at this point is undergoing the same crisis of faith that Mulder must deal with after the events of this episode arc; she recovers hers in "Redux II" whereas Mulder takes a bit longer to reestablish his. Scully generally does get with the program much faster than Mulder does, she deals with the loss of her biological daughter Emily in season five in the episode "All Souls" just a few short months after Emily's death, whereas it takes Mulder years to come to grips with the loss of Samantha. She comes to overtly believe in Mulder's aliens by the beginning of season eight and probably is well on her way to it as early as the beginning of season seven, whereas Mulder doesn't accept the divine until the closing scene of the series finale "The Truth."

"Gethsemane" is book-ended by two very different Scully reactions; in the beginning she studiously avoids telling Mulder that her cancer has metastasized so as to not use her personal condition to distract him from his quest. At the end she switches gears entirely and tells him that his quest is the underlying reason for her cancer which has the effect of killing his belief entirely. Scully tells her brother Bill that she is responsible to what's important to her so perhaps by the end of the episode after all the information they have gotten from Kritschgau she believes that it's time for Mulder to stop his running after aliens and she's willing to play the trump card that she would ordinarily never use.

REDUX

"I have held a torch in the darkness to glance upon a truth unknown. An act of faith begun with an ineloquent certainty that my journey promised the chance not just of understanding, but of recovery. That the disappearance of my sister 23 years ago would come to be explained and that the pursuit of these greater truths about the existence of extraterrestrial life might even reunite us. A belief which I now know to be false an unformed in the extreme. My folly revealed by facts which illuminate both my arrogance and self-deception. If only the tragedy had been mine alone, it might have been more easy tonight to bring this journey to its end."

In a typical *The X-Files* bait and switch in the fifth season opening episode "Redux" it is revealed that instead of committing suicide as is suggested in "Gethsemane," Mulder shoots and kills Department of Defense employee and spy Scott Ostlehoff. In order to buy time, he and Scully set it up to appear as though Mulder has killed himself in an attempt to allow him more freedom to move around unwatched. Of course it doesn't really work because Cigarette-Smoking Man doesn't buy the suicide lie for a minute. What CSM doesn't know is that Mulder is under surveillance in the first place. CSM, a bit put out that he's been kept in the dark on this, tells the First Elder that he created Mulder and that he has always been able to keep him in check. Even though CSM apparently doesn't known anything about the surveillance in Mulder's apartment, he does know that Scott Ostlehoff is the man Mulder shoots and that

Mulder now has his key card which suggests that CSM has Mulder under surveillance of some kind too.

The First Elder also tells CSM that Mulder is an asset, but that they have underestimated his fragility concerning Scully. CSM says that he never underestimates Mulder. CSM knows exactly how important Scully is to Mulder which is why he frequently uses this attachment against him. Mulder seriously considers suicide; since his biggest concern when he speaks to Kritschgau on the phone is Scully's cancer and whether he is the reason for it this is likely to be the real catalyst for his desolation. CSM lets Mulder leave the Department of Defense (DoD) with the cure for Scully's cancer. Since he knows what Scully's death would do to Mulder it's unlikely he ever planned to actually allow her to die; by giving Mulder the opportunity to obtain the means for her recovery he further cements the bond between the partners, which in turn gives him even more leverage with Mulder.

Through the phone records Mulder finds with Ostlehoff, he and Scully figure out that there is a conspiracy tie to the FBI. In what seems to be the Consortium's standard operating procedure they again leave damning evidence at risk of being found; perhaps an illustration of their hubris. Scully suspects Skinner of being the mole whereas Mulder doesn't; probably due to his knowledge of Skinner's actions in "Zero Sum" and his motivation.

In "Gethsemane" Kritschgau mentions bio-weaponry in his dissertation to Mulder about what he believes to be going on. In "Redux" he expands on the tale and puts it into context with the cold war. The Consortium and the military's main purpose with the testing is to build a better soldier or weapon by combining the best qualities of the alien and human physiology. It all continues to suggest that there are aliens, but not in the way Mulder expects; they're not really little green men from outer space at all–instead it is a collective consciousness generally contained in a virus that imparts certain capabilities onto its host in a successful symbiotic relationship.

Dr. Vitagliano tells Scully that the chimera cells begin to divide when exposed to bovine fetal serum and begin somatic development. In other words, the cells start to create something which appears to be the first reference to the virus using existing biomaterial to create a biological body; an idea that foreshadows the main story line of the movie. Based on the results of the Southern Blot, Scully believes that she is exposed to the virus and these chimerical cells during her abduction and that it ultimately causes her cancer.

The thing that Mulder wants most desperately of all is the cure for Scully's cancer. Finding Samantha comes in after that–in fact, she isn't even mentioned until "Redux II" and CSM has to bring her up. Mulder doesn't even try to find information on Sam while he is at the Pentagon in the Consortium's Mecca of information–he is completely focused on Scully.

REDUX II

At the beginning of "Redux II" Mulder finally realizes that Scully is in the process of dying. Luckily Skinner keeps him from being arrested when he flips out at the hospital. Scully can't be saved until Mulder puts aside his personal quest and focuses on her–a lesson he should take more to heart since his ability to help save the world revolves around the same concept. Scully's big brother Bill really doesn't like Mulder and initially tries to characterize him as nothing more than a part of Scully's work. Later he wants to know if Mulder thinks it is all worth it and calls him a sorry son-of-a-bitch. Even though Mulder tells Bill that it isn't worth it he still continues down the same path after Scully's recovery; he hasn't yet learned that the end never justifies the means.

"Redux II" also explores the miracle of Scully's remission. The real agent of that miracle is left open to interpretation; is it the chip or the divine? The Walk-Ins have saved her before and have a vested interest in saving her again. Since Cigarette-Smoking Man allows Mulder to obtain the chip, it may be that the devil (metaphorically-speaking) has as much of a hand in saving her as they do. CSM obviously wants to keep Scully alive–he even allows Mulder to find the means to save her before he offers him the deal. He may simply be attempting to earn Mulder's trust or loyalty, but if so, he could easily have Scully killed once Mulder turns him down. Instead Samantha is the carrot that CSM feels comfortable taking away when Mulder refuses to join him.

Mulder later tells Scully that the deal with CSM could have saved his life in a way. There are two ways of understanding that statement; one, that his life is tied directly to Scully's and losing her would have ended a major part of his own and two, that taking the deal would have kept him out of prison, which would also be a sort of death for him. Since he decides to turn down the deal after he realizes that Blevins is the mole but before Scully's cure is confirmed, it's likely to be the latter instead of the former.

CSM most likely wants Mulder to work for him because Mulder is the one he wants to take over his role as king. CSM also knows about the prophecy that is referenced in the seventh season opening episode "The 6th Extinction" and has probably mistaken the reference to the man who will save the world as referring to Mulder and wants to control the outcome by controlling the man. The prophecy specifically states that the Messiah's father will play a major role in influencing the direction things go – a role Mulder is later supposed to play with William.

It is hard to tell if this Samantha believes herself to be the original. In retrospect, it's likely that CSM has a clone made like the ones in "Herrenvolk"– only without the additional genetic manipulations–for his own use. He has some kind of emotional tie to the real Samantha–either that he is her biological father or wants to be her figurative one–and may have created this one to fill the void left when the Walk-Ins took the real McCoy as seen in the seventh season episode "Closure."

Skinner is set up to take the fall for Mulder. Perhaps this is done to protect Mulder without giving away the real mole. If so, it would appear that the First Elder is also continuing to protecting Mulder to a degree. The First Elder also attempts to have CSM assassinated. CSM has more lives than Mulder does, which is saying something. As the representation of the devil; he can't really be killed by something as mundane as a bullet or a shove down the stairs. Even his body's rejection of Mulder's genetic material couldn't quite do it; it ultimately takes total immolation by a missile after he's willingly passed on the king's mantle to Mulder in the series finale "The Truth."

"Redux II" is the first time that Mulder's two families–the original represented by Samantha and the new represented by Scully–collide. The return of Samantha alone, neither in "Redux II" nor later in "Closure," restores family to Mulder; it only frees him to find his true one.

CHRISTMAS CAROL

The episode arc "Christmas Carol"/"Emily" centers on the idea of family and its importance when Scully experiences the mythological loss of her own in the discovery and the subsequent death of her biological daughter Emily and the continued estrangement between her and her brother Bill. It also appears that Mr. and Mrs. Sim aren't very happy with each other. There is an important subtext running throughout this arc about parents again choosing to sacrifice their daughter (who this time is connected to Scully) for the good of the Project. In addition, it appears that, yet again, the mother of the child is opposed to the decision although in this case at least, she is willing to be paid off. In the end it destroys the family and child; this is Scully's version of Mulder's family saga.

Emily is the genetic product of the Consortium and has autoimmune hemolytic anemia (this is a condition where the patient's immune system attacks and destroys the red blood cells– shades of the retrovirus) which requires daily injections of what appears to be the green goo. The Walk-Ins using Melissa's voice and a series of symbolic dreams want Scully to rescue Emily from the tests. There are aliens working on this project, but they are probably hybridized drones like the Jeremiah Smiths and the Kurt Krawfords. Emily is *not* a clone of Scully or she would be identical to her at that age, not Melissa and is different in some way from the other drones since they do not have the lethal medical issues that she does.

The social worker assigned to Emily's case plans to recommend the rejection of Scully's application for adopting Emily because Scully is single and has never had a long-term relationship. Her work is also cited as time-intensive and dangerous and the social worker isn't sure that Scully will be able to put Emily first. Scully says that she has questioned her priorities since she was first diagnosed with cancer and that she no longer feels the same fear about committing to someone that she once did. Given the eventual importance of placing William over the quest this is an important lesson for Scully (and Mulder) to learn.

In the end however, she goes too far and tries to keep William from his destiny by putting *him* up for adoption.

Scully calls Mulder and then hangs up on him–she's not quite ready to be completely open with him yet and chooses to not share Melissa's phone calls with him. Of course Mulder avoids telling Scully that he has her ova so he hasn't learned that particular lesson yet either. One thing that is fairly consistent about Scully's characterization up through the events of sixth and seventh season "Biogenesis"/"The 6th Extinction"/"Amor Fati" arc is that she is far more willing to maintain an open mind about paranormal events when Mulder is not involved. She typically keeps this openness hidden from him.

Tara really puts her foot in her mouth when she unintentionally hurts Scully with her comments about life being somehow less meaningful without a child. While perhaps not a popular ideology in today's world, it is important in *The X-Files* mythology; especially in light of William's later conception and birth and Scully's archetypal role of the mother.

Since on the show and in myth dreams are often means of communication used by the divine. In this episode arc the dreams seem to be connected in some way to the events just prior to them. Scully's dream about the rabbit is about her fear that loving something too much is suffocating to it and that she will ultimately lose it. It may explain why Scully never makes any demands of a personal nature of Mulder and why she never uses her pregnancy or William as a means of holding onto him. It may be that she fears she can't love him without that somehow stifling his quest and kill him or that which makes him special. The rabbit is a symbolic representation of Mulder and since Bill is antagonistic towards him it makes sense that Scully would dream he is after her bunny. Based on her later reaction to Diana and what she represents–someone who, outwardly at least, has not stifled Mulder and his beliefs along with the feelings Scully later voices in the movie; it is likely that she believes her science is also suffocating him. Perhaps it is this fear and not the fact that they are partners that keeps Scully from seeking a romantic relationship with him. Scully also dreams of Roberta Sim in the casket and herself as a child; a probable metaphor for the loss of Scully's family by placing her in the position of Emily in relation to Mrs. Sim.

Scully's next dream is her conversation with Melissa. Missy tells her that there is no right or wrong and that life is a path that will take Scully where she is supposed to go. She also tells her not to mistake the journey for what is really important–the people she will meet along the way and how she will affect their lives and vice versa. Since Melissa is a product of the Walk-Ins, this is their message to her; the journey isn't as important as the people involved. Again here's the notion that people are the most important thing not the events.

EMILY

"It begins where it ends... in nothingness. A nightmare borne from deepest fears, coming to the unguarded. Whispering images unlocked from time and distance. A soul unbound, touched by others but never held. On a course charted by some unseen hand. The journey ahead promising no more than my past reflected back upon me. Until at last I reached the end. Facing a truth I could no longer deny. Alone, as ever."

The episode "Emily" cements Scully's mythological identification with the Virgin Mary and the mother archetype. It also hints at Mulder's identification as the father of the messianic child; both in his fiddling with the Joseph figure from the nativity scene and probably more importantly in the role he attempts to take on with Emily even though he's not too thrilled with the idea of Scully adopting her. In his father role he completely blows a gasket with Dr. Calderon. He calls him a medical rapist and wants *"everything to help that little girl."*

Mulder tells the judge that Scully's ova were extracted during her abduction—something he apparently never mentions before in order to protect her; a tendency he still has in the series finale "The Truth." What he still doesn't let her in on is the fact that he has a vial of them stored away somewhere—something he finally spills the beans on in the eighth season episode "Per Manum."

A tumor like mass is taking over Emily's body, killing her normal tissue as it goes. It is basically replacing her natural circulatory system with toxic green blood. It appears that the virus or the green-goo environment is somehow vulnerable to a hyperbolic chamber or more likely the high oxygen content. Perhaps oxygen plays a role in the corporeal aliens' vulnerability to the puncture at the back of the neck. It's unlikely that the green substance that Mulder steals from the nursing home would help Emily. It may have stabilized her physically, but ultimately would only allow her unnatural transformation to continue. At this point Scully probably makes the best decision by letting Emily die—or not interfering with the natural course of things.

Emily is a characterized as the miracle that is never meant to be, whereas William is the one that is. The big difference is that Emily isn't created out of love and William is. Perhaps the Walk-Ins don't merely take Emily as they do Samantha because it is necessary for Scully to experience these events to prepare her for her ultimate role in William's life. It may be a test of sorts to see if Scully will put Emily first and she apparently passes muster. It is interesting to note that Emily *does* have a soul—she's seen going to the light later in "All Souls." Perhaps this is when the Walk-Ins finally rescue her. Scully's cross the symbol of her connection to the divine and her faith returns to her yet again.

The elderly women who give birth to these babies remain in their beauty sleep because they are most likely infected with the virus which puts them into the suspended animation first seen in the fourth season episode arc "Tunguska"/ "Terma." It appears the black oil medium protects the host from the dangerous brain illness that Mulder experiences in at the end of the sixth and the seventh season.

Scully's final nightmare seems to imply that her greatest fear is to remain alone; her life nothing more than a reflection of her past. It could either be a reference to her immediate past or to her failed past lives/cycles; a concept that is hinted at again in the fourth season episode "The Field Where I Died" and in the ninth season's "Hellbound." Scully wants to be alone with Emily while she's waiting for her to die; at this point her worst nightmare is

coming true–she is alone. Until she allows Mulder to become fully involved, things are not in balance; this final unity is ultimately the resolution to the Mulder/Scully story or would be if they didn't make the wrong choice in the end.

POST-MODERN PROMETHEUS

The fifth season episode "Post-Modern Prometheus" is a contemporary retelling of Mary Shelley's *Frankenstein's Monster* and acts as a metaphor for the fundamental moral of the mytharc. The story is about the difference between the natural and the unnatural and that you can't always judge a book by its cover; sometimes the true monsters aren't the Great Mutatos, they are the men who create them.

The Great Mutato with his two faces represents the dual nature of the monsters created by the Consortium. While he is horrible to look at, he has more humanity than his creator, a vain and ambitious man. The Great Mutato is created not out of love, but because of Dr. Pollidori's ambition and hubris. When he doesn't live up to the doctor's standards he is discarded as worthless.

The farmer, representing the father archetype, rescues the Great Mutato and raises him as his own son. The Great Mutato yearns to experience a mother's love and idolizes Cher because of her role in the movie *Mask*. She represents unconditional love that cares not for outward appearances but for what lies underneath, highlighting the importance this kind of love and acceptance plays in *The X-Files* mythology. Dr. Pollidori kills his father–the farmer–in a fit of rage when he figures out what he did, he then tries to pin the murder on The Great Mutato; something that's fairly easy to do with the simple townsfolk, but not so easy with Mulder and Scully. The metaphor here is that Mulder and Scully have the capability of looking below the surface and seeing the truth underneath, which is probably the reason they are chosen to be William's parents.

In "Post-Modern Prometheus" Prometheus' fire comes in the form of genetic knowledge. Man playing the creator with little thought to the consequences. The farmer in a misguided attempt to create a suitable mate for the Great Mutato, inseminates local women with the only genetic material he has available to him, chicken, pig, and goat. The resulting children take on subtle characteristics of their fathers while still remaining outwardly human—these are the representations of the hybrids. Their hidden genetic genesis allows them to be welcomed into the community, whereas the Great Mutato with his horrible face is not.

There is quite a bit of symbolic imagery in the episode. The victim's houses are shrouded with a tent that apparently no one notices; a metaphor for society's ability to willfully not see that which is hidden in plain sight. Mulder and Scully have no problem seeing Pollidori's house tent and all, although once inside they too are overwhelmed and fall victim to the same opiate as the victim does.

Dr. Pollidori's wife has an odd sense of interior design; their house is strewn with greenery and little lights. On first appearances it looks like paradise, but in reality it's a house full of sadness and longing; a possible metaphor for the world of the divine, obviously the aliens want something they don't have even if it looks like they have it all.

The townsfolk all appear to be infatuated with the idea of the Jerry Springer show and welcome Mulder and Scully with open arms for as long as they buy into the monster story. As soon as it gets out that Scully believes it to be a hoax the tide turns against them.

However, once the townsfolk hear what The Great Mutato has to say they realize that he is really no different than they are and understand that he too deserves to be loved. Shaina and Dr. Pollodori's wife give birth to their own Great Mutatos and get to realize their dream to be on the Jerry Springer Show; a nice metaphor for the idea that once true unification between alien and man occurs (as it does in William) the dream is realized.

BAD BLOOD

At first glance, the title "Bad Blood" appears to be referencing the vampire theme, but it also refers to the tension between Mulder and Scully. The episode gives the viewer a peek inside their heads and illustrates three important things; first, how they each see themselves, second, how they see each other, and finally their insecurities about their attractiveness to the other. Here it is all about their partnership, the vampires are merely the backdrop against which it is played out. It's important to remember that the two of them are in the middle of a bit of a tiff (that bad blood), which affects their perceptions. Scully is upset that Mulder dismisses her theory throughout the case whereas he's angry that she doesn't want to go in the first place. Add to that the underlying tension of Scully's attraction to Sheriff Hartwell and you have memories blown way out of proportion—as is typically the case in the series narrative. Ultimately what Scully wants most of all is for Mulder to see her as smart, capable and interestingly enough, sexy. Mulder on the other hand, just wants desperately for Scully to stay with him and admire his intelligence. Their recollections are colored by their own biggest fears.

In both cases their perception is that they are the significantly less dominant partner which is fascinating because in reality they are both such strong and assertive personalities. Perhaps their normal general bossiness is overcompensation for what they each internally perceive to be a weakness. In Scully's mind Mulder cavalierly orders her around and she meekly acquiesces every time. In reality, she does tend to end up going along with him, but she normally puts up a bit more of a fuss about it first–although certainly not as much of one as he apparently thinks she does. Mulder on the other hand, sees himself as overly conscientious of her feelings and respectful of her opinion, not to mention somewhat frightened of her.

Perhaps their recollections aren't truly how they really see their own actions as much as how they want the other to see them. Scully wants Mulder to know that his behavior makes her feel like a useless tagalong whose only purpose is to do autopsies and Mulder wants her to know that she scares him or probably more accurately that he's afraid she'll finally refuse to follow him. Interestingly in his version Mulder has no sense of humor, which is one of his defining traits. Maybe this is an indication that this defense mechanism is mostly subconscious for him.

In Scully's version Mulder never shuts up. He interrupts her constantly and he is extremely sarcastic about her thoughts on the case. In fact, he has a hard time even remembering her name when introducing her to Sheriff Hartwell. He also embarrasses her in front of the sheriff by telling her to get those little legs moving. He is cracking bad jokes and he maliciously withholds information. All things designed to make her contribution look less than important. He does behave this way all the time, but this is a complete exaggeration of how he normally goes about it. These are the traits that make Mulder, Mulder after all and normally, while Scully may find them irritating, it's unlikely she sees him as quite this callous. The important thing here is that in Mulder's mind he isn't dismissing Scully and her contribution at all. Internally he does respect her opinion and isn't nearly as sure of his own theories as he lets on.

In Mulder's version, Scully is a raging bitch. She's sarcastic and really unenthusiastic about the case. She is easily distracted by the sheriff and uses guilt against Mulder. She's constantly rolling her eyes at his comments and only considers him as an afterthought in her diatribe. Again, behavior designed to make it clear that she doesn't want to be there and more importantly with him. Like Mulder, she does do this, only no where near to this degree. These too are the traits that make Scully, Scully. Again, in her mind, she went along with Mulder without much fuss and is not angry at him at all.

Mulder also has the additional insecurity that she'll find an attractive man and leave him. Perhaps this is a left over fear from her fiasco with Ed Jerse in "Never Again" or it could be Mulder's insecurities over Scully going off to find a normal life. There is also a peek at Mulder's guilt complex where Scully's concerned when she tells him that she does it all for him. No doubt, he'd rather she did it for the work instead.

Finally, the most interesting thing is their attempts to highlight in themselves those traits they feel the other finds attractive. First, in Scully's version, Sheriff Hartwell is extremely interested in her and finds her smart and alluring. He's almost fawning over her and in her retelling she makes sure to point this out to Mulder. In addition, this guy isn't afraid to use her first name, something Mulder rarely does. Conversely, in Mulder's version he's the smart one while Sheriff Hartwell is a raging idiot and ugly to boot. Mulder makes sure that in his retelling Hartwell is extremely impressed with his intelligence and competence. Mulder even exaggerates a negative physical trait (the overbite) in Hartwell that he himself has.

In Scully's version Mulder barely registers the fact that Hartwell is attracted to her at all, whereas in his version he only notices her mooning over the sheriff who seems relatively indifferent to her. In his mind, Mulder is extremely nice to Hartwell, yet when we see them together in reality he is sarcastic and dismissive. He leaves Scully with Hartwell because even though he is bothered by her interest in Hartwell, as far as he's concerned the feelings aren't reciprocated so he isn't worried anything would actually happen. Until Agent Doggett, Mulder seems to have somewhat of a blind spot in this regard. He always appears to be surprised when another male actually shows romantic interest in Scully. While Scully on the other hand always assumes every female is out to bag Mulder.

One final thing, in the scene where they're waiting to talk to Skinner, Scully is trying to take care of Mulder by fixing his tie and telling him to say he was drugged. Mulder tells her to stop it yet he makes sure his tie is straight and the first words out of his mouth are "I was drugged!" He'd like for Scully to believe he's indifferent to her attentions, yet in reality he takes them very seriously.

In the end the vampires are nothing like their press. They don't burn up in sunlight, crucifixes have no effect, and they have no fangs. Similarly, Mulder and Scully are not like they think they are. Mulder isn't nearly as indifferent to Scully's contributions as he appears to be and Scully isn't as cold or unfeeling as she comes across as. Ultimately, their outward behavior is not necessarily indicative of what they're really thinking or feeling.

PATIENT X

Before the exploration of space, of the moon and the planets, man held that the heavens were the home and province of powerful gods, who controlled not just the vast firmament, but the earthly fate of man himself. And that the pantheon of powerful warring deities was the cause and reason for the human condition, for the past and the future and for which great monuments would be created on Earth, as in heaven. But, in time, man replaced these gods with new gods and new religions that provided no more certain or greater answers than those worshipped by his Greek or Roman or Egyptian ances-

tors. And while we've chosen now our monolithic and benevolent gods and found our certainties in science, believers all, we wait for a sign, a revelation. Our eyes turned skyward, ready to accept the truly incredible, to find our destiny written in the stars. But how do we best look to see? With new eyes or old?...

The X-Files frequently makes use of an opening voice over in the mytharc episodes. The peculiar wording and rhythm takes these commentaries out of the story proper and into the realm of narrations of mythic ideas that usually pose pertinent questions. The one that opens "Patient X" is no exception and the mythic idea it suggests–rather pointedly–is the notion of the aliens as the divine and the question it poses is about the nature of those gods; is it the current Judeo/Christian monolithic and benevolent version or the more capricious one of the Greek/Roman and Egyptian pantheons?

"Patient X" and its sister episode "The Red and the Black"are heavily influenced by mythology, from Cassandra's name, to the constellation Cassiopeia that she draws in fingerprints on her window. In Greek myth, both Cassandra and Cassiopeia are being punished by the gods due to their actions, Cassandra for rejecting Apollo's romantic overtures and Cassiopeia for her hubris in saying she was more beautiful than the Nereids. In "Patient X" Cassandra Spender is referred to as an apostle and a prophet. She's trying to tell Mulder that the aliens are here to bring a message about a coming age of supernatural enlightenment–echoing almost verbatim the Walk-Ins message in the second season episode "Red Museum." Her fate, like that of her Greek counterpart (whose prophecies are true in the myth by the way), is that Mulder refuses to believe her.

On the other hand, Cassiopeia through one fateful and vain act brought down Poseidon's wrath on the land in the form of a monster. The oracle tells Cephas that the monster could only be appeased by the sacrifice of Cassiopeia and Cephas' daughter Andromeda. Cassiopeia, however, does eventually becomes a constellation, or in *The X-Files* terms, starlight. Perhaps the message here is that man's hubris brings down the wrath of the gods in the form of the aliens, and are then required to sacrifice their daughters (the Consortium's sons and daughters as seen in "Two Fathers"/"One Son") to appease the monster. However, all is not lost, like Cassiopeia, man can eventually achieve a reunion with the divine in the form of starlight. Another connection may be in the Colonist/fallen angel angle and the parallel to Satan's hubris.

One of the women on the panel Mulder attends actually voices the Grail question; it isn't whether the aliens are here or not, the question is *why* they are here. In other words, who does the Grail serve? Mulder should be trying to understand the true natures of the aliens and their various agendas instead of merely trying to prove they exist. It is only in the wisdom gained from *this* understanding that he can hope to make the right choice when the time comes.

Like most of the mytharc episodes perception plays a large role in the various points of view on display; from Mulder's theory on the military's involvement, Scully's confusion, Jeffrey Spender's skepticism, to Cassandra's total belief in aliens. The Consortium is portrayed in "Patient X" as a scared group of men desperately seeking a vaccine against that which they don't understand. Meanwhile Krycek's true nature is on full display, from his cruel torture of Dmitri to his bid to grab total power.

THE RED AND THE BLACK

The episode "The Red and the Black" continues to be heavily influenced by existing mythology, this time it's the Navajo Monster Slayer and Child of Water twin myth that Cigarette-Smoking Man speaks of in his letter to Jeffrey Spender. The difference is that this myth is directly referenced by a character and its relevancy is affected by that character's perceptions or misperceptions; whereas the oblique narrative references like names are not. There are definitely significant similarities between *The X-Files'* mythology and the Navajo twin myth, the problem is that CSM has made the wrong connections. He identifies Child of Water with Spender, when Scully is the much more apt personification. The Navajo twins are not at odds with each other as Spender and Mulder are; instead they work harmoniously together as partners. In "The Red and the Black" however, the younger and subservient twin begins to balk at following her partner until she can better understand what has happened to her. Interestingly Mulder is willing to risk having his life's work invalidated in order to keep her with him.

The other possible misconception is who exactly the real monsters in this myth are. As seen in "The Post-Modern Prometheus" they aren't who the viewer may think. Generally on the show, men are the real evil. Krycek is the one who is torturing the boy and who is trying to grab all the power. The freighter ship Star of Russia is a nice metaphor for the fear of what happens on the alien ships during an abduction. Krycek's violence comes back on him and his boon is stolen by the conniving Marita. Sex is a powerful thing in myth and here it is used against the shadow hero by the feminine aspect or the anima.

The color red is used symbolically a lot on the show, here it represents the human element from the color of the envelope CSM sends his letter off in to the color of the helicopters and one of Scully's suits. Black represents the alien (or divine) aspect in the color of the black oil. The title may also be a reference to a Marxist propaganda film of the same name. McCarthyism is addressed again in the next mytharc episode "Travelers" and works well as a metaphor for the Colonist/Consortium or Alien/Human fear factor. Which is the bigger evil; Communism or the men in power who would use accusations of complicity as a means of punishing or eliminating those whose beliefs don't toe the party line?

Scully undergoes regression hypnosis and remembers her time in the night place or on the bridge at Ruskin Dam. However, the show has made a point of showing that regression hypnosis is an unreliable means of recovering memories; from Mulder's multiple versions of Samantha's abduction to the various perceptions in "Jose Chung's From Outer Space." There is no way to know for sure who is behind the second ship, the only real clues show up later in the sixth season episode "Two Fathers" when Cassandra relates this latest abduction as a bad experience and she echoes the rhetoric about evil aliens that the Consortium is known to intentionally place in abductees' memories. Cassandra also ends up in the Consortium's hands as a full hybrid–something that the Colonists have no knowledge of; which strongly suggests that she isn't taken by them. It seems most likely that Quiet Willie is sent with Cassandra in order to report back to the Consortium the location of the next holocaust. They then send out one of their captured UFO's, or even a top secret military aircraft like Mulder postulates, to destroy the Rebels and protect their interests. It's unlikely that the Consortium believed that Quiet Willie alone could have any real hope of stopping the events or even surviving them without help.

On a side note; the term holocaust is probably intentional and is meant to point out that the Rebels are racial purists like the Nazis, who would use a form of genocide in order to achieve their agenda. They are not the good guys and want to exclude mankind from the divine.

Finally, the Consortium decides to hand over the captured Rebel in order to maintain their collaboration with the Colonists, however, the alien bounty hunter that comes for him has to sneak onto the airbase and then has to disguise himself as Quiet Willie in order to get the Rebel off again. If he's from the Colonist faction, that shouldn't be necessary. It's more likely that this particular bounty hunter is from the Walk-Ins and is acting in his avenging angel persona. He's stopped by the arrival of the Rebel ship and Mulder's attempt at intervention. Mulder experiences the same memory loss as Scully does and they are back at square one. Mulder has now begun to question his new theories based on Krycek's warning and Scully has begun to question her new theories based on Spender's.

TRAVELERS

The episode "Travelers" is about disenchantment and becoming a target by evil when one attempts to escape it. In a continuation of a theme from "The Red and the Black" Communism and McCarthyism witch hunts are the metaphors used in this episode to illustrate these ideas. In *The X-Files* universe McCarthyism was used to disappear those men who have become disenchanted with the Project; which explains why Bill Mulder continues his participation for as long as he does. He doesn't want to put his family in danger; which is kind of ironic given that he later allows Samantha's abduction and the subsequent horrible tests that are performed on her. He even turns a killer lose so that a greater truth can someday be revealed; an event that later sparks Mulder's interest in the x-files–although this directly contradicts the mytharc episode "The End" that reveals that Diana is the one who introduces Mulder to the x-files. Generally when there is a contradiction of this magnitude it's intended to illustrate that one of the accounts is wrong; but which one?

The hybridization experiments are in full swing as far back as 1952. Since the Consortium doesn't have access to the alien DNA until the 1970s it appears as though they are using some kind of insect/spider like thing and are attempting to actually graft it onto a human instead of creating a genetic hybrid. The episode "Lord of the Flies" in season nine revisits the descendents of the original human subjects.

Arthur Dales is a great illustration of what Mulder could become without Scully's influence; a point Dales later makes in the sixth season episode "Agua Mala."

Mulder is apparently married to someone in 1990. Either it is Diana since it's revealed in "The End" that they are together when he leaves the Academy and she doesn't leave for Europe until 1991 or he is having an affair with her during his marriage. He is also smoking–which is a metaphor for the dark side on the show. Perhaps this is a precursor to "Amor Fati" and the idea that Diana can only lead Mulder down the wrong path.

THE END

"The End" with its chess imagery focuses on the strategic maneuvering and sacrifice ideology that is the MO of the Consortium and often times, Mulder. The child prodigy Gibson Praise with his telepathic abilities acts as catalyst for the episode's various conflicts and as the bone being fought over. The NSA wants him dead, probably because he can tell the difference between an alien and a human; a skill you'd think would be particularly advantageous for them to have–unless they're really concerned about his ability to also recognize a super soldier.

Mulder believes that Gibson has an active God Module and may be the answer to all unexplained paranormal activity–in other words, everything contained in the x-files. Based on later information the virus also has something to do with the God Module which may suggest that all paranormal phenomena can be traced back to it. Gibson isn't infected with the virus–he does, however, have the brain physiology that would allow for a safe infection without the resulting brain illness that Mulder later suffers from in the seventh season. Gibson is not the same as William however, he is only a human with the necessary physiological changes; he is missing the actual incorporated alien sentience and duality that William has.

"The End" also introduces Special Agent Diana Fowley the personification of what Mulder's believes is his ideal woman, who is a female carbon copy of him in many ways. She is an apparent ex-chickadee of Mulder's who wants to pick up where they left off. She is with Mulder from the time he leaves the Academy until she is assigned to a terrorism unit in Europe after she becomes a FBI agent herself in 1991. The two of them work together on paranormal cases and have a romantic relationship of some kind–possibly marriage or an extra-marital affair based on the wedding ring Mulder is seen wearing in the episodes "The Unusual Suspects" and "Travelers," both set during the same time period. She is doing some strategic maneuvering of her own and hints that perhaps she would make a better partner for Mulder–with her like mind–than Scully. Mulder seems glad to see her and while he defends Scully's contribution, he is obviously still taken with Diana and a two-fold betrayal begins; Diana's betrayal of his lingering feelings for her and his betrayal of Scully's feelings for him. The Diana Fowley development also begins to show that Mulder isn't above sacrificing Scully, at least emotionally, in order to get what he wants: this is a parallel between CSM and his sacrifice of Cassandra for Teena and Mulder's close brush with sacrificing Scully for Diana.

Diana is ultimately working for Cigarette-Smoking Man and is almost killed probably to more firmly cement Mulder's feelings for her. She is shot while guarding Gibson, yet later recovers in record time by the sixth season opening episode "The Beginning" which suggests the work of the renegade alien bounty hunter that cures Teena Mulder in the fourth season opener "Herrenvolk."

Gibson appears to trust Scully the most–he doesn't really have much reaction to Diana at all and a fairly lukewarm one to Mulder. He does keep needling Mulder about his thoughts though. Gibson is probably responding to the fact that Mulder and the various Consortium/NSA types–Diana included–sees him as an object to be used or destroyed. Scully, on the other hand, seems to take a maternal interest in him, which fits her role as the good mother archetype. It's interesting to note that in the ninth season Mulder winds up becoming more of a father to Gibson than he ever is to William. Gibson probably doesn't recognize Diana's treachery and warn Mulder and/or Scully because she is kept pretty much in the dark and her only real orders may be to rekindle her relationship with Mulder– something Gibson does pick up on. But then again, so do Mulder and Scully for that matter–Diana isn't exactly subtle.

When it comes to *The X-Files'* female characters, the narrative relies heavily on the Madonna/Whore dichotomy or the light and dark sides of the various female archetypes. On one end of the spectrum there is Dana Scully, who is consistently identified with the Virgin Mary; the ultimate Madonna. She is virtuous, loyal, and steadfastly on the side of good. On the other is Diana Fowley who is identified as a fallen woman who sells her soul to the devil (Cigarette-Smoking Man) and attempts to lead the hero astray.

Nowhere is this dichotomy more evident on *The X-Files* than when it comes to sex. Sex in this narrative is removed from real life and takes on a mythological slant. It is portrayed as either dangerous or as a healing and creative power depending upon who a male character's *female* partner is.

Diana Fowley and Marita are both portrayed as sexual manipulators. Fowley uses sex either abstractly or concretely to lead Mulder around and even wields it against CSM. It is unlikely that it is coincidental that the actress chosen to play her exhibits extreme physical sexual characteristics. Fowley looks like she's a centerfold poured into a suit and Mulder's preoccupation with pornography probably sets up his vulnerability in this regard.

Diana's pursuit of Mulder sexually is clearly in the context of her working for CSM. She ultimately wants something other than a relationship with him and sex becomes a tool of manipulation. Mulder's "Amor Fati" dream illustrates this idea fairly well; she's clearly in league with CSM to distract Mulder and it is the opportunity for sex with her that removes his literal handcuffs, but metaphorically enslaves him with perhaps less tangible but no less binding ones. Diana represents the temptation that would derail Mulder's real destiny–not his so called quest, but the conception and birth of the boy on the beach.

Marita also attempts to use sex to manipulate Mulder in "Tunguska," and in this case it doesn't work (unless Mulder is the quickest gun in the West). She is more successful later in the fifth season episode "Patient X" when she uses her feminine wiles against Krycek in order to kidnap the black oil infected boy. She has sex with Krycek as a means to an end; it isn't about love at all. From a mythological standpoint the reason is all-important. In both cases, these women and their sexual natures are used in a negative way against men. The reason that the manipulation is female in nature is because it is she who stands to gain something extraneous and self-serving from it–not the male.

Even Teena Mulder is tainted with this stigma and is branded an adulteress. All of these women ultimately pay the price for their indiscretions; Diana is killed, Marita is subjected to an infection with the black oil and subsequent horrifying tests, and Teena is stricken with a disfiguring disease. They all find a sort of redemption in the end, but only Marita escapes with her life, saved in the series finale "The Truth" by the two men she used.

In almost every case, the males of the mytharc are shown to have weaknesses in this area. Mulder most certainly does–he is completely vulnerable to the helpless woman syndrome and sexually predatory females can easily manipulate him. Skinner succumbs to a prostitute in "Avatar" and again *she* pays the ultimate price. Even bad boys Krycek and CSM aren't immune and have been tricked by sexually predatory females.

On the other hand, Scully is portrayed as virtually sexless–until she has sex with Mulder. In this case, sex creates William–intended to be the ultimate healing for mankind. Scully could quite easily use sex to get her way with Mulder and Skinner, but she never does. Even when she finally does make the naked pretzel with Mulder it is presented as the ultimate in non-pressure as is the pregnancy that results from this union. She has to come to terms with Mulder's reality–no normal life–before they can consummate their relationship–not the other way around.

In a gross generalization, Scully ends up being the stereotypical male ideal. She is beautiful, strong, loyal, not prone to emotional outbursts, smart, and she is ultimately sexual without pressure or apparent expectation and it is all on Mulder's terms. She even ultimately ignores his infidelity after having fed his ego by fighting over him. She chooses him unconditionally when confronted by a rival for her affections. She is mythologically tainted somewhat with the Ed Jerse affair in "Never Again," yet even here as in "Milagro" she is seen as a healer not a destroyer.

Mulder, on the other hand, is allowed to stray, but the female is always portrayed as the guilty party. She is the one who tempts him and while he may pay an emotional price for falling–the women are ultimately the ones who are punished.

Scully has a negative reaction either professional or personal jealousy or insecurity over Diana. A reaction that–just like Mulder's odd secretiveness about his past with Diana–isn't incidental; it has meaning in Mulder's journey. Diana is the seductress who would tempt Mulder from his real destiny–not his quest, his role as William's father. An interesting side note is that over the course of the show Mulder usually refers to the work as starting when Scully joins him on the x-files. However, according to "The End" he actually works on them with Diana for a while before Scully arrives. He seems to discount that time as unimportant; which suggests that he probably doesn't achieve a great deal.

By the events in "The End" Jeffrey Spender has come to really dislike Mulder and vice versa. CSM uses this antipathy to recruit Spender in an attempt to make Spender the son (mythological heir) that he originally and ultimately intends for Mulder. CSM seems particularly evil in this episode and between his use of Diana as a wedge between the partners and his destruction of the x-files office with fire; he makes a concerted effort to bring Mulder down emotionally.

Mulder and Scully end up in deep trouble professionally by the conclusion of "The End" and are reassigned, although this time–unlike during the beginning of the second season– they remain partners.

THE FIRST THEATRICAL MOVIE

The X-Files theatrical movie plays like a fairy tale complete with a damsel in distress to the handsome prince who rescues her from eternal slumber with a kiss. The most interesting aspects of the film is that while the text is all about killer plagues and terrifying aliens, the subtext in the form of symbolic imagery is all about fertility, rebirth and transformation. Corn and bees are both strong mythological fertility and rebirth symbols and the 'jiffy pop poppers' look for all the world like huge breasts springing from Mother Earth. There are dark womb-like caves in both Texas and Antarctica that open into light.

Scully's time in the cryopod in the Antarctic ship strongly invokes birth imagery with the fluid and the umbilical like tube that feeds her. She emerges naked and wet and Mulder encourages her to breathe. Scully's emergence from the chrysalis is a premature rebirth however, just as Mulder's is in the eighth season episode "DeadAlive." She's taken on divine aspects, but has not become fully divine.

The cryopods as chrysalises bring to mind not only metamorphoses of a caterpillar to a butterfly, or more importantly the changing of the same organism to a different and higher form. Perhaps the transformation from human to alien isn't the appropriation of the biomaterial of one sentience by another, but a transcendence of the original. In other words, the resulting alien is the same person in a different form. The ship is a sort of underworld and its entrapment in the frozen wasteland of Antarctica a means to slow or stop the progress of the transformations of the dead.

There is also a clear parallel between Vergil's telling of the myth of Aristaeus. Orpheus destroys Aristaeus' beloved bees as a punishment for his role in Eurydice's death. However, unlike Orpheus, Mulder is able to rescue his beloved from the depths of Hades and bring her home. The same theme of rescue from Hades is repeated in the myth of Demeter (the goddess of mother earth and fertility whose symbol is an ear of corn) and Persephone. The Demeter/Persephone myth is one of rebirth and is connected to the transformation of the earth from the cold and barren winter to the warm and fertile summer. For part of the movie, Scully is in Texas in summer and for part she is in Antarctica in winter.

Oddly, given all the work the Project scientists have apparently done with it, Well-Manicured Man tells Mulder that the Consortium knows very little about the virus, which may support the idea that they are operating under a huge misconception. They believe that the transformative strain represents a mutation that creates a brand new life form, when instead it becomes apparent in the sixth season opening episode "The Beginning" that this is merely the manner in which the Grays–who generally represent either the older virus or the Walk-Ins–reproduce or possibly how a host becomes a higher entity. There is a huge contradiction in the Consortium's apparent ignorance about the metamorphic aspect of the virus and their access (and perhaps control) of the ship which is full of partially transformed people. Generally on the show this type of contradiction means something is not as it seems.

The ship appears to be slumbering. Apparently CSM has some control over it as he uses it to store Scully and the other infected people. What exactly he's doing isn't made clear, although it is obviously that he at least knows about the viruses' ability to transform, the bodies clearly show the developing aliens. The ship only awakens once the vaccine is administered by Mulder. Instead of destroying the aliens, it brings them along with the ship back to life.

The juvenile Grays appear to operate under pure id or instinct, whereas the fully adult Grays act more like ego and superego or from the fully integrated self. The appearance of the aliens even changes from the large muscular vaguely lizard-like form with its deadly claws to the more gentle and benign Gray of popular folklore. However, based on other information given throughout the mytharc, the Grays seem to want to escape this type of reproduction or transformation and become more humanlike or perhaps return to their prior human form bringing their new found abilities along with them.

Well-Manicured Man also tells Mulder that his father allows Samantha to be abducted so that she can become an immune hybrid, which would have given her the ability to survive the coming holocaust. Here is one more example of the end justifying the means–an ideology that never succeeds on the show. The twist is that this immunity that the Project is trying so hard to achieve, may in fact, be a very bad thing. At the very least it would render those who have it unable to participate in the coming transformations and new age. The Consortium is operating out of fear–mostly in their loss of control and power–and ignorance; always a bad combination for finding the real truth.

The film introduces Dr. Kurtzweil, an OB/GYN–not surprising, considering the reproductive aspects of the Project–who previously worked with Mulder's father. Kurtzweil's plague rhetoric may be as far fetched as his other ramblings. He understands a small part of the whole and twists it to meet his conspiracy ideology or perceptions of reality.

The writers employ a metaphor for the dialectic nature of the Mulder and Scully partnership in the crossroad they come across on their journey to find the tanker trucks. The answer lies in neither the left (Mulder) nor right (Scully), but somewhere in the middle. Mulder comes to this realization when Scully resigns and plans to leave. She believes that she only holds him back, whereas he understands (at least for the remainder of the film) that her science saves him and makes him whole. He realizes that he can't find the truth alone. Strughold says at the very end that one man can not fight the future—he's right, but Mulder and Scully together can, especially since William can become the saving grace if he is allowed to meet his destiny.

Mulder is willing to literally go to the ends of the Earth to rescue Scully. Strughold decides to take away from Mulder that which he can't live without by having her infected by the virus and turning her over to the Colonists. How the Consortium manages this is something of a mystery. Unless the bee is working in conjunction with them, its trip on Scully's collar and the timing it shows (when CSM has an ambulance standing by) stinging her seem to be a huge coincidence. Since the virus can control its host, it is possible that the bee is acting intelligently and that this virus represents some kind of enslaved version carrying out CSM's wishes.

The ship in Antarctica is unlikely to be a Colonist ship since according to the fake Samanthas in "End Game" they don't show up on Earth until the 1940s. The ship however, contains people from as far back as the last Ice Age. Given the Rebels agenda of racial purity, it is unlikely that their form of the virus would use the biomass of another race or species to create a new body. So this ship belongs to either the oldest strain like in "Tunguska" or the Walk-Ins. Since the virus in "Tunguska" does *not* cause the transformation and the vaccine does at least cause it to go dormant, the Walk-Ins are a better bet. Once it has awakened by the vaccine the ship even appears to aid Mulder in his rescue of Scully with well-timed blasts of steam that hold off the marauding juveniles.

The ship comes alive and appears to free itself from its prison of ice. As it flies away it returns to a pure energy state taking all of the transformed people with it. Mulder's faith is again restored when he witnesses the ship and its contents first hand; although he too allows fear of the unknown or different to color his perceptions. Of course, the nasty behavior of the juveniles probably doesn't help.

THE BEGINNING

And so begins the season of Mulder's temptation and near loss of the one who makes him whole. Somehow Mulder forgets (as is his tendency to do) just how important Scully is when faced with Diana and her seductive charms. Season six shows us a truely punkish version of Mulder during the mytharc episodes all due to the influence of someone who is pretty much a reflection of himself. Diana and Mulder are alike from the credulous belief in the paranormal to the very act of betrayal of the one who matters the most. Cigarette-Smoking Man is using both of their credulous natures to manipulate them into furthering his agenda; Diana is just a more willing participant. Diana and Spender are assigned to the x-files and Mulder initially accuses her of stabbing him in the back. However, he later changes his tune when she begins her campaign of being everything that Scully isn't. Mulder has already begun to discount Scully's science–the very thing that he says saves him in the movie–in favor of the unquestioning belief that Diana offers. Mulder's inherent hubris is rearing its ugly head and in typical mythological form, nearly becomes his downfall. The first casualty is his trust in Scully, the foundation on which their partnership is built and the Syzygy (Jung's divine couple) archetype is seriously threatened.

The company Rousch–first mentioned in the fifth season opening episode "Redux"–is back and is apparently working with the mutated virus strain from the movie. One of the Rousch scientists is infected by the virus and gestates an alien–or transforms–in just 12 hours. The gestation is hastened by heat, the hotter the better, and the final stage is the appearance of the more recognizable Gray.

Unfortunately Scully's tests fail to show that the virus creates anything. Assuming she obtains the sample from the bee this is probably really important. Perhaps the bee isn't carrying the same strain of virus that causes the lizard alien. There just isn't enough of a time lapse between when the Consortium finds the new strain in Texas to when Scully is infected by the bee for it to have been incorporated into its venom via the pollen. Not to mention that the new strain would most likely have begun to gestate within the bee for a brief time, until the biological material has been used up. Instead Scully is infected with an enslaved form that is working for the Consortium's agenda. The claw on the other hand is left behind by mistake and comes from the Walk-Ins, and in a way tells Scully something very important from their perspective, if she only makes the right connections. Here is proof that the aliens aren't really extraterrestrial–unless we all are–and that they share the same genesis as all other life on Earth.

The Consortium now has Gibson and is doing horrible things to his brain, probably the same harvesting of genetic material that CSM later tries with Mulder in the seventh season opening episode arc "The 6th Extinction"/"Amor Fati." CSM also tries to use him to find the missing alien and Gibson leads him away from Mulder and Scully as they investigate the unfortunate (or fortunate, depending upon how you look at it) Rousch employee's home. Gibson tells CSM that he knows that CSM is afraid of him because he could destroy him by what he is and knows; yet another example of the fear of the unknown driving the Consortium and in this case CSM's agenda.

Gibson at first appears to have the virus in his system, however, later Scully amends that and says that he instead has remnants of the same DNA as that of the virus and the claw. Gibson isn't William however, since he is missing the incorporated alien sentience. Perhaps he's a genetic throwback with the original remnants of the virus' early interaction with man; humans have a lot of junk DNA in our genome, left over from our evolutionary history. It is also possible that he's like the Mexican nationals in the eighth season episode "Vienen" and is immune, which would then preclude him from the symbiotic relationship. The vital piece of information here is that at some point in our evolutionary past mankind either came from the aliens or shared a relationship with the virus (our Garden of Eden so to speak).

Scully's good mother archetype is in full swing in "The Beginning." Mulder isn't exactly acting like the good father–he wants to use Gibson the same way CSM does–albeit not as brutally. Scully wants to use him in a way too and tries to make Mulder see that he's their best chance at corroborating Mulder's story. Gibson calls her on it. Again, Gibson doesn't seem all that interested in Mulder or what he wants or thinks. That disinterest later disappears once Mulder stops trying to use him and begins to care for him as a father figure.

Mulder and Scully end the episode assigned to Assistant Director Kersh and investigating domestic terrorism. They are told to have no contact with the x-files or Diana and Spender.

TRIANGLE

The episode "Triangle" is essentially a metaphor for the mytharc using the same basic premise as *The Wizard of Oz*. The framework is the Nazis, World War II, the atomic bomb and the Bermuda Triangle instead of the secret tyranny of the Consortium and the threat of alien colonization. The characters play, not themselves, but one of the roles in the real narrative.

In Mulder's World War II experience/dream the Queen Anne is a luxury liner on a cruise from America to England. It's the beginning of the war and the Germans have boarded the ship because they believe its carrying munitions for the allied forces. The ship is a metaphor for mankind's progress and carries all of the necessary ingredients to save humanity, if steered in the correct direction. The ship's journey from America to England or the expected route would only prove disastrous for mankind. It's only in turning the ship around and heading into the unknown that true freedom is found and the world is saved.

The Nazis– which generally represent the Rebels–are led by Cigarette-Smoking Man with his son Jeffrey Spender as his right hand man and mouth piece. There is also an anonymous assassin–who looks suspiciously like Krycek–who does his dirty work. They have a spy in place in the flirty female singer played by Kersh's assistant. What the Nazis really want is to find the secret that the ship is carrying which may be a clue as to what the Rebels are really after. This is interesting in that the Consortium generally has an agenda that mirrors the Colonists, however, CSM is usually scheming outside of this and his true agenda may be a mirror of the Rebels instead; human racial purity with all the goods.

Skinner is a German SS officer who originally appears to be working with CSM, but is, in fact, undercover for the Americans—generally the role Skinner usually plays but may also represent the renegades like Jeremiah Smith.

The idealistic captain Yip Harburg (a nod to the lyricist who wrote *Somewhere Over the Rainbow*) represents Mulder in his quest to defiantly stand in the way of evil. Unfortunately like Mulder, all of the captain's heroics, while sounding great, do nothing to actually stop evil and he ultimately dies a meaningless death at least as far as saving the world goes. Luckily in the series narrative Mulder apparently has nine lives and gets to keep coming back to try again yet in the end he does the same thing at the trial and is only saved from death by his friends.

The deck crew fishes Mulder out of the ocean and accuses him of being a German. They drag him to the captain who interrogates him, slaps him and locks him up in his office after Mulder tells them exactly where they are and tries to explain what he believes to be happening. Here Mulder gets a taste of his own medicine. He plays the part of the Walk-Ins, who know what's going to happen and try desperately to tell someone (a representation of himself in fact) how to stop it to no avail. The captain, in his paranoia, can't tell the good guys from the bad and locks Mulder away, just as Mulder has locked away the myriad entreaties of the divine.

The song that's playing during Mulder and Spender's fight is *Bei Mir Bist Du Schon* and the specific lyrics heard are something about "the fairest in the land" and could be a subtle hint about the Walk-Ins' divinity. Mulder steals Spender's uniform and then attempts to impersonate a Nazi, perhaps a reference to the Walk-Ins frequent use of the alien form.

Kersh and the Jamaican engine crew, who represent the Colonists, have taken real control over the ship's course by commandeering the steering mechanism. They just want to go home regardless of the consequences. They aren't bad guys, but their efforts aren't going to help the cause either and will ultimately be futile. It is interesting that amongst all the players they are the only group that wants to hear what Mulder has to say and may be a reference to the fact that the Colonists ultimately aren't opposed to the Walk-Ins agenda or are at least willing to consider it.

The oblivious passengers represent mankind and dance the night away while the Nazis take over the ship. It isn't until CSM starts shooting them that they even realize that they are in danger and it isn't until the different crews show up that they overcome their fear and join in the battle against the real villains–a possible metaphor for the idea that only in uniting with the aliens can mankind hope to win against the real evil that would control their lives.

Scully shows up in two incarnations; as a 1939 undercover OSS officer who's in charge of protecting the scientist Thor's Hammer and in her normal, albeit desperate, role as the one who pulls Mulder's butt from the fire–or water in this case–and brings him home safe and sound.

Only Scully's role in the story is basically the same in both narratives which is to protect both the scientist and to steer the journey back to the mystical. Ultimately it falls into her hands to turn the ship around after Mulder leaves. Mulder as the Walk-Ins tells Scully what she needs to do and then has to leave it in her hands to accomplish it, just as the Walk-Ins apparently do in the real narrative. The scientist, or Thor's Hammer, is William. He can be used by either good or evil depending upon Scully's success in turning the ship back to the spiritual.

Mulder (as the Walk-Ins) is willing albeit reluctantly to watch innocents die in order to protect the truth or the ultimate goal of transformation. Only when Scully is threatened does he break down and even then he stills tries to cover it up. It isn't until The Scientist makes the true correct and moral choice– though it would appear to be the dangerous one at first– do the crew and passengers show up to begin the battle against the Nazis which suggests that William's messianic choice will ultimately decide the fate of mankind.

Mulder never actually does anything beyond run beyond trying to convince everyone what his or her reality is (which he initially has completely backward) and get beat up for it. It's Scully, Skinner, the crew, and the passengers that actually resolve anything and Scully is the one who ultimately convinces everyone they need to turn around. She's the one who knows the Scientist's true identity and is protecting him–at least until Mulder shows up and appears to blow everything (but really doesn't, instead it is the catalyst for the change). The Walk-Ins role is to guide but it is up to man to do the real work.

The journey's resolution in "Triangle" requires that Mulder as the Walk-Ins, recognize the true path and get Scully to take it. They do not want the ship to return to America–or the initial mistake, but instead, realize that the journey has to come full circle and return to its historic roots and the wound must be healed. Scully succeeds in the eighth season and William is born. Unfortunately Mulder (as himself) is still too attached to his personal self-glorifying quest and leaves to chase his version of the truth; the family or balance is ultimately destroyed once more and the cycle must begin again.

Scully is the one who goes through the biggest change throughout the nine seasons of the show–from the pure skeptical scientist to the emotional believer. In "Triangle" in Scully's sojourn through the FBI she's desperately searching for the necessary science that will find and save Mulder. She takes on pretty much everyone of any importance to do so and her accusations to Skinner is the catalyst for his help. His reward is a kiss, which may allude to his motivations for helping Mulder and Scully in the first place.

After running the gauntlet in order to get the information she needs to locate Mulder she eventually finds him face down in the water (seemingly drowned) after having searched an empty ghost ship. When he wakes up he tells her that *she* saves the world because she believed him and then tells her he loves her. To which she replies *"oh brother"* and leaves. It is an interesting bit, remember in Mulder's "dream," he plays the role of the Walk-Ins, not himself and his comments are relevant to both.

There are a few important details in the real Scully's big scene. First, like Mulder, she accidentally hurts an innocent bystander while trying to get information on how to save him. She also inadvertently blabs in front of CSM, or basically tells CSM that Mulder is up to something, again just like Mulder does with The Scientist. Even the message that she gets when she tries to call Mulder– *"The cellular customer you're trying to reach is not responding"*–is important; this is at the height of the Fowley fiasco and Mulder isn't responding to Scully at all; hence her response to his declaration of love.

Finally Scully tells Mulder *"There's no place like home"*; which is the ultimate truth.

DREAMLAND I & II

"Once upon a time, there was a guy with the improbable name of Fox Mulder. He started out life happily enough, as these things go.

He had parents who loved him, a cute kid sister. He had a roof over his head, got all his flu shots, had all his fingers and toes and aside from being stuck with the name 'Fox' which probably taught him how to fight— or not— he pretty much led a normal life. But the worst thing by far — the biggest kick in the slacks this kid Fox ever got — was what happened to his sister. One day, she just disappeared. Now, Fox buckled down and worked his butt off. Graduated top of his class at Oxford, then top of his class at the FBI academy. None of that hard work made up for his sister, though. It was just a way of putting her out of his mind. Finally, the way I figure it, he went out of his mind and he's been that way ever since. Fox Mulder pissed away a brilliant career, lost the respect of supervisors and friends and now lives his life shaking his fist at the sky and muttering about conspiracies to anyone who will listen. If you ask me, he's one step away from pushing a baby carriage filled with tin cans down the street. But now, all that's going to change."

Another aspect of the Jungian side of *The X-Files* is the writers' use of the shadow archetype; the repressed needs that come into direct conflict with the expressed ones. In the episodes "Dreamland I" and "Dreamland II" in using Mulder's and Morris Fletcher's reactions to having lost their notion of home and family the narrative deals with the idea of these contrasting aspects by illustrating both parts of Mulder as hero.

The episode arc begins with Scully asking Mulder if he ever wants to just get out of the car, in other words, embrace the more sociologically accepted notion of home and family. The events in "Amor Fati" indicate that he does truly desire these more concrete trappings of home and family in his own way. The "Dreamland" episodes illustrate what his reality of these notions actually is, which is something far more abstract. That's not to say that the house in the suburbs can never happen, it's just that family means a great deal more to him than that, the house itself has no meaning beyond a place to keep his stuff. The idea of home and family in *The X-Files'* myth represents balance and harmony.

Even though Mulder has the prime opportunity to find the answers he has sought for so long he chooses instead to put his energies into finding a way home and back to his commitments. Fletcher, on the other hand, is running away from his responsibilities. Fletcher has the outward family with his wife and two kids, but his internal sense of family and commitment is non-existent. Mulder, on the other hand, is the epitome of the single and unattached bachelor on the surface, yet he has a fully internalized sense of family–even if he doesn't yet recognize it–and is struggling to return to it. Family to Fletcher is the over-mortgaged house, dissatisfied wife, and kids who hate him–all the external trappings, but none of the heart. A horror that he wants desperately to escape from until that heart has been restored. Mulder isn't so much actively running away from the house in the suburbs as he is running back towards his notion of home and family which *is* about the heart and has nothing to do with the surface trappings. Fletcher returns to a presumably more love-filled family whereas Mulder returns to an apartment that has mysteriously acquired a bed, a visual symbol of the coming consummation of his family.

Fletcher's sexuality is completely externalized. He is trying to score and it doesn't much matter with whom. First he hits on Kersh's secretary who is more than willing and then on Scully, who is not. Mulder, on the other hand, has completely internalized his libido by utilizing pornography and dreaming about Scully. Even when faced with the sure thing that Fletcher's love-starved wife represents, he chooses to have his potency questioned before having sex just for sex's sake. It isn't that Mulder doesn't have desires (and problematic vulnerabilities to them), he does, it is that he has chooses here not to actively pursue them just for sex's sake. Joanne spends the episode either attempting to get Mulder, as Fletcher, to live up to his marital responsibilities or throwing him out of the house and castigating him for not being the perfect husband. Scully, on the other hand, is either yelling at Morris, as Mulder, for ignoring his quest in favor of sex or is desperately trying to find a way to bring Mulder home. Joanne is only worried about her desires just as Morris is about his, whereas Scully is most concerned that Mulder focus on what she perceives to be his highest priority, her feelings aside.

Even though Fletcher knows the skinny on what is really going on he could care less; all he wants is out of his old life even if that means stealing Mulder's. He is in charge of fabricating the lies that are being disseminated to the public and is using the Lone Gunmen to perpetuate them. Mulder, as you would expect, only wants to find the truth and pass that on, but not at the expense of living a lie. Fletcher is a butt-kisser who uses any means (or lie) necessary to get on Kersh's good side and reap the rewards. He is more than willing to sacrifice Scully's career in the process.

Mulder, on the other hand, immediately gets into trouble with the authorities and ends up in jail. He does not want Scully to lose her job and is willing to risk full exposure in order to achieve that end. Since trust is non-existent, Joanne expects lies from Fletcher and isn't all that shocked at Mulder's odd behavior. She just thinks he's going through a phase. Scully, on the other hand, isn't able to figure Fletcher's behavior out at all and it's this very lack of trust that ends up being the catalyst for her realization that he isn't Mulder.

THE RAIN KING

The theme of "Rain King" is that truth has the power to transform. Repressed truths are dangerous, whereas an acknowledged one, like requited love, can heal the king and the wasteland and bring about the world somewhere over the rainbow. In this episode there is another reference to the *Wizard of Oz* and the notion of home.

Sheila and Holman are clearly metaphors for Mulder and Scully. The question is who represents who? The obvious choice is probably Mulder/Holman and Sheila/Scully. In many ways this works, however, there is a stronger connection between Scully/Holman and Mulder/Sheila; especially at this particular point in the overall narrative.

Like Sheila, Mulder has become infatuated with someone (Diana) who tells them what they want to hear and mistakes that for love even though it is a tenuous attraction at best. They are both completely clueless about the real and undying love that is right in front of their noses. Both mistakenly believe that *they* are the one who has the power to transform the world.

Holman the scientist personifies Scully's insecurities over the reaction of the object of their affections to the truth of their feelings for them. Holman stays in Kroner, Kansas for the same reason Scully remains on the x-files, to stay near the one they love. It is Holman and the force of his love that can truly bring back life to the drought-stricken farmers, just as it is ultimately Scully who can produce the child that can save mankind. Of course Holman can't do it alone, just as Scully can't.

Daryl and Cindy also represent aspects of Mulder and Scully. Daryl personifies Mulder's narcissism and self-absorption. He is all too quick to walk away from the woman who truly loves him (and is willing to stay with him for who he is and not for who he thinks he is) for the one who has something he wants; whether that's Sheila and her money for Daryl or Diana and her beliefs for Mulder.

Cindy, on the other hand, personifies Scully's possessiveness and her blind belief in Mulder's kingship. When Daryl walks away from Cindy he becomes crippled again just as Mulder would become crippled if he loses Scully. In perhaps a bit of foreshadowing, Daryl asks Cindy why she's so good to him, when she forgives his betrayal.

Perhaps Mulder doesn't gaze at Scully and is perfectly happy with their friendship exactly the way it is. Then again, so is Sheila *until* she realizes the true depth of what Holman feels for her and where the transforming power really comes from.

HOW THE GHOSTS STOLE CHRISTMAS

In this episode Mulder's desire to spend Christmas Eve with Scully causes him to dig up an x-file. There appears to be a personal meaning to him in this case given the parallels between Lyda and Maurice and Scully and Mulder. The story certainly sounds familiar. War with the Nazis and plague, interestingly neither of these actually kill Maurice or Lyda–they do it to themselves. In the story the gods (note the plural) couldn't protect them from the dangers of the world. According to the story Maurice and Lyda's main concern is remaining together.

The idea of unconscious yearnings comes up frequently in this episode so there are likely lots of symbols that represent subconscious desires. The first one is Scully's car keys. They disappear and she's hooked into staying with Mulder even though it's against her New Year's resolution. Keys and locks are common sexual dream and myth symbols. Jung sometimes thought that the appearance of keys is a metaphorical representation of the solution to a problem. Locks can represent repressed content–sometimes sexual. Given the fact that the plot revolves around a "lover's pact" and loneliness, it's likely to have some sexual or romantic connotations, however, the likely bigger meaning is that the keys represent Scully's life outside of the x-files. Mulder denies taking her keys, although given his reaction to Maurice's accusation that he did, it is likely he's guilty.

Once Scully is in the house (which represents Mulder's quest), Mulder repeatedly ignores her pleas to help her get out. She's locked in and can't escape and Mulder makes no attempt to help her do so. Interestingly as Scully begins her droning rationalizations she becomes caught up in what's going on and no longer tries to leave. Mulder essentially leads her upstairs while appearing to ignore what she's saying or her contribution.

In the foyer the grandfather clock is keeping perfect time and represents the journey. Mulder and Scully have to resolve the conflict by midnight in order to escape unscathed. They have a limited amount of time in which to accomplish what they need to.

Lyda and Maurice are yet one more instance of the dead trying to guide them. They are trying to tell Mulder and Scully about their partnership and where the problems are which isn't surprising given the timing of this episode; the sixth season is a very troubled time for the partnership.

Next up is the stairs. Jung believed that stairs are symbols of psychic transformation in which the unconscious is brought into conscious awareness. Mulder and Scully climb up the stairs (with Scully rationalizing the entire way), which lead to the door to the library. The library with it many books represents the unconscious mind, hence its use as the central location. The ladder is probably just another symbol for the same thing. Mulder can't find the ladder until Lyda brings it back. He then climbs down into the library where she tries to get him to recognize his unconscious motivations. Mulder tells her somewhat wistfully, that he and Scully aren't lovers.

The library also houses the two buried and desiccated corpses. Lyda even specifically calls the corpses Jungian symbolism. They represent the final outcome if Mulder and Scully can't make their transformations.

The fireplace represents strong emotions; love, hate; desire. When Mulder and Scully first enter the library, the fire has just gone out. Lyda later relights it while discussing Mulder's motives.

The brick walls are pretty obvious. These are the barriers to Mulder and Scully's ability to escape loneliness. Maurice tells Mulder to go find his partner and change his life by going through the brick wall—which Mulder can't consciously do. Maurice even specifically asks Mulder if the brick wall is real or only in his head. Scully runs into a brick wall also, so the same obstacle is in place for both of them.

Maurice and Lyda's psychoanalyses of Mulder and Scully are pretty much on target. As in "Never Again" and "Bad Blood" they are over emphasized to make a point. The episode seems to suggest that Mulder's motivation is primarily loneliness, thus his creation of the brick walls. In any case Mulder most certainly is narcissistic and self-righteous. In light of the ultimate futility of his quest, Maurice's negative comments seem to be on target.

For Scully, it's codependency and conflicted yearnings. Perhaps she does just want to prove Mulder wrong, but tellingly, later at his apartment she seems to think that this is the only reason Mulder wants her around, which explains why she does it.

When fake Mulder finds Scully and starts shooting at her and telling her that they have to die, Scully tells him that she doesn't believe what he's saying. Later when the real Mulder tells her that they haven't been shot, she believes him which allows them to escape. Scully knows that the real Mulder wouldn't hurt her and in the end it is her trust and belief in him that saves them.

In the foyer, Scully tells Mulder that she's not going to make it. He tells her *"not without me you're not"* which is a good metaphor for the idea that Mulder and Scully are much better together than apart. Scully can't make it out of the quest without Mulder and vice versa. Also, they both have to make their way out of the subconscious in order to make it.

Just a side note, this may be coincidental, but Lyda's gun shot wound is in her abdomen which may represent Scully's loss fertility, where as Maurice's is in his head, which may represent Mulder's later brain illness.

S.R. 819

> *"Every minute of every day we choose. Who we are. Who we forgive. Who we defend and protect. To choose a side or... to walk the line. To play the middle. To straddle the fence between what is and what should be. This was the course I chose. Trying to find the delicate balance of interests that can never exist. Choosing by not choosing. Defending a center which... cannot hold. So death chose for me."*

"S. R. 819" is about the influence of the shadow or dark side of one's nature. In this episode Krycek infects Skinner with little nanobots in order to control him with the Palm Pilot O' Death. They are made of carbon and multiply by splitting and build little dams and valves and control the blood supply in Skinner's body. Skinner has now become a slave to his shadow or the personification of his darkest impulses. Krycek gives Skinner notice that he (as the shadow's influence) holds the key to whether the AD lives or dies. Skinner feels that he has always played things safe–straddled the fence as it were. He apologizes to Scully for it–yet reverts back once he's out of immediate danger. It isn't until Skinner finally takes a stand after Mulder is abducted that he actually achieves anything of value.

Senator Matheson is back and is connected to S.R. 819 which is a health bill that is supposed to be for funding health care in Third World countries, instead it appears to be a front for sending new technology out of the US. Somehow Krycek is involved and at first appears to want the bill passed; however, it later seems as though he orchestrated the events in order to stop it. He infects Dr. Orgel and possibly Senator Matheson with the nanobots too.

Since the technology is being exported to Tunisia which is where Strughold is, the Project must be involved in some way. It could mean that the nanobots are connected to the creation of the super soldiers. It is possibly a fail-safe mechanism to control them since they are pretty indestructible; however, given the super soldiers later apparent ascendancy to control in the ninth season it doesn't work. The Tunisia connection should have later raised flags for Mulder when Scully reveals Diana's connection to it in "Two Fathers." Again Mulder ignores the evidence that doesn't mesh with his own personal world view.

TWO FATHERS

"This is the end. I never thought I'd hear myself say those words after all these years. You put your life into something... build it, protect it... The end is as unimaginable as your own death or the death of your children. I could never have scripted the events that led us to this. None of us could. All the brilliant men... the secret that we kept so well. It happened simply, like this. We had a perfect conspiracy with an alien race. Aliens who were coming to reclaim this planet and to destroy all human life. Our job was to secretly prepare the way for their invasion. To create for them a slave race of human/alien hybrids. They were good plans... right plans. Kept secret for over 50 years, ever since the crash at Roswell. Kept secret from men like Fox Mulder. Plans that would have worked... had not a rebel alien race come to destroy them. Had not my own son chosen betrayal. Or chosen to betray more wisely."

Apparently the deal that the Consortium struck with the Colonists to help create a slave race of alien/human hybrids has been in existence for 50 years, since Roswell. The whole slave race angle doesn't really jive with what we've heard directly from the aliens however. The deal is really just a smokescreen both sides use to cover up what they are really doing.

Like Dr. Secare in "The Erlenmeyer Flask," Cassandra is successfully turned into an alien/human hybrid. She bleeds green and can heal instantaneously–including her previous paralysis. She does not appear, however, to be controlled by the alien sentience in any way. Since the doctors are wearing gas masks she must be infected with at least the retrovirus and not the non-lethal version that Dr. Charne-Sayre is working with in "Terma." The fact that the Consortium fears that the Colonists will find out about her condition strongly suggests that they have nothing to do it in the first place.

Mulder has been slacking off and not doing his job. He seems completely disheartened at this point, something CSM had been striving for all along. It certainly makes him more vulnerable to Diana and her lies. He even buys into CSM's story later in "One Son."

Scully asks Mulder to talk to Cassandra because of what she can tell them about Scully's experiences. He reluctantly agrees and Cassandra tells him that the black oil is the aliens' life force (or more likely the virus it contains since the oil itself isn't anything special) and is infecting all other life-forms. Cassandra's attitude about the aliens has made a drastic change since the events of "Patient X." Her new reasoning is much more in line with the lies that the Consortium spouts and along with the Colonists' ignorance of her condition suggest that they are not the ones who abduct her from Ruskin Dam. We also learn that her first abduction is the same night as Samantha's on November 27, 1973. Cassandra also tells him that Samantha is still out there with the aliens; this is an interesting belief, given what is shown later in "Closure" and Cassandra's role in Samantha's life at that point (surrogate mom). Samantha *is* still out there with the aliens, but not in the manner that is suggested here.

The Rebel faction does not kill Cassandra in the train car when they have the chance. According to CSM they spare her in order to expose the Consortium. It would appear that they want them exposed to the Colonists; this only makes sense if Cassandra does not represent what the Colonists are after and is a threat to them; a direct contradiction of the hybrids for slaves story. However, what is the Rebels motivation? They are at war with the Colonists, so perhaps this is a divide and conquer tactic.

CSM's name—or at least one alias—is C.G.B. Spender. He has now moved beyond the nameless and becomes more human. His inability to kill Cassandra highlights this change. He doesn't love her, yet has a connection to her that he can not sever.

CSM tells Diana outright that he purposely ruins Mulder—if she loves Mulder so much why does she agreed to help CSM continue this campaign? CSM also tells Diana that he has chosen Spender to replace Mulder, probably as his heir apparent (the new king mythologically-speaking).

The Rebels apparently wear some kind of mask in order to disguise themselves or shape-shift. These Rebels at least do not have toxic blood, although it is the green goo.

Krycek appears to realize that the Second Elder is really a Rebel and is covertly passing on the Consortium's plans to him during his presentation. The false Second Elder appears to be trying to get the Consortium members to join forces with the Rebels; yet Krycek is subtlety working against that. CSM doesn't want to join in with the Rebels either and also knows that the Second Elder is a fake.

The "Two Fathers"/ "One Son" narrative arc is hell on the partnership. Scully's trying to keep Mulder interested in the events going down, but he seems distanced and not all that involved until she finds the box of stuff on CSM and Bill Mulder. For some odd reason Mulder seems surprised that the Project is still going on. CSM also acts as though this is the first time Mulder has made the connection between him and Bill Mulder. Mulder and CSM seem particularly prone to living in their own realities that don't necessarily jibe with what they should know given their previous experiences.

Krycek is nervous about Jeffrey Spender and the ice pick weapon–is this a clue about his true nature or just a subtle reminder that it's a weapon? There is no indication later on that Krycek is anything other than human, so this nervousness seems odd too. Krycek is also falsely painting CSM as a great man even though we know he believes anything but. He seems to be manipulating Spender into turning against CSM and it works.

ONE SON

"Two men, young, idealistic — the fine product of a generation hardened by world war. Two fathers whose paths would converge in a new battle — an invisible war between a silent enemy and a sleeping giant... on a scale to dwarf all historical conflicts. A 50-years war, its killing fields lying in wait for the inevitable global holocaust. Theirs was the dawn of Armageddon. And while the world was unaware, unwitting spectators to the hurly-burly of the decades-long struggle between heaven and earth, there were those who prepared for the end; who measured the size and power of the enemy, and faced the choices: stand and fight, or bow to the will of a fearsome enemy. Or to surrender — to yield and collaborate. To save themselves and stay their enemy's hand. Men who believed that victory was the absence of defeat and survival the ultimate ideology... No matter what the sacrifice."

"One Son" is about betrayal. There is the Consortium's betrayal of the Colonists and how the Rebels' later use that to lead the Consortium members to their own destruction. There is also Diana's betrayal of Mulder (though still unrecognized by him) even in the face of his continued belief in her, regardless of the facts. In addition, there is Krycek's insidious betrayal of CSM by orchestrating his son's betrayal and CSM's resulting final betrayal of Jeffrey by shooting him. Finally we have the near miss of Mulder's ultimate betrayal of the work and mankind when he decides to join his enemies in order to save those he loves, Diana, Scully and Samantha. Only Scully's swift kick in the butt by refusing to give up with him stops it a role she plays again in "Amor Fati."

Mulder does want to take Scully to El Rico with him—although, interestingly enough, he waits until he has invited Diana first before letting Scully in on the fact that the world as they know it is ending. Since time is of the essence you'd think that he would get on the phone immediately and clue Scully in. Perhaps this is meant to illustrate just how defeated he has become, he's just sitting there waiting for Fowley to arrive so he can take her to the base and save his own butt, an action that goes against everything he appears to believe in. Of course he does the same thing at the beginning of the ninth season when he abandons Scully and William to protect himself, so perhaps it's an essential part of his character. It is ultimately the cause of his failure.

It is revealed what has been happening to Marita since her betrayal of the Project in "The Red and the Black" and it isn't very pretty. She tells Mulder about the vaccine although he should already know about this from his conversation with Well-Manicured Man in the movie; again Mulder's memory is apparently very selective.

Jeffrey Spender is apparently clueless about the fact that Diana works for his father since she's there when he tells his mother that he is protecting her from CSM and doesn't appear to be concerned that she'll report back. There is no information in the FBI files about Diana's work in Europe. She spends a lot of time studying the MUFON women and makes weekly trips to Tunisia during her assignment there. Mulder continues to be blind to the evidence of her duplicity, probably because it doesn't fit his preconceived notions; a hubris that will be his ultimate downfall. Apparently Diana is in the know about the prophecy since she has access to the black book that spells it out in "Amor Fati." Mulder even asks Scully to not make his affiliation with Diana personal, although this seems extremely out-ofline given her connection to the MUFON women.

Mulder's voiceover tells us that the Consortium's agenda is to collaborate with the enemy, in this case the Colonists, in order to survive no matter what the sacrifice and is again another reference to the supposed deal. According to CSM his reason for wanting colonization to begin is so that the Consortium can save their own butts and get those they sacrificed in the deal back. This is really odd since he doesn't have anyone left to *get* back and the deal itself seems to be bogus. At this point in the narrative we could argue that he wants Samantha returned—but after the events of "Closure" it becomes obvious that he already knows she is no longer with the Colonists.

It appears that the first priority of the Rebels is taking out the Consortium, not averting the so called colonization. They do steal the well-spring—the alien fetus—before Krycek can prevent them from doing so; this would certainly curtail any addition genetic experiments using their DNA and possibly the future of the super soldier program in keeping with their racial purity agenda.

CSM makes an interesting comment to Mulder during their discussion in Diana's apartment. He tells Mulder that the Consortium does what they have to so he (Mulder) can survive and that Bill Mulder failed to realize that; another possible reference to Mulder's role in the fulfillment of the prophecy that CSM knows about. CSM also tells Mulder that he will live to see his sister's return. He can't be referring to Samantha coming back with the others because he *knows* she's dead so he is either lying yet again to Mulder or he may be referring to William if he believes that the messianic child is a reincarnation of Samantha. There's a certain mythic eloquence to this given how Samantha's soul was initially betrayed by her father only to have Mulder (as this soul's new father) given a chance to choose the opposite and right the previous wrong. Unfortunately he ultimately does the same thing that Bill Mulder did and betrays her once again.

THE UNNATURAL

David Duchovny's episode "The Unnatural" is a metaphorical journey through a central theme of *The X-Files* myth; both humanity and the ability to transform into the divine are found in the ability to focus on love and the unnecessary things and *not* in grand quests and fame. Josh Exley doesn't want to be a *famous* man; he just wants to be a man. Dales tells Mulder that baseball is the key to life; the Rosetta stone to his understanding the truth he seeks.

Josh wants to become human because his people (the aliens) lack the ability to laugh and do unnecessary things–something Mulder and Scully seem to have difficulty with too. Dales tells Mulder that he can turn chicken salad into chicken spit and that if he were to give Mulder a piece of ash, Mulder would want to make a cathedral when all Arthur really wants is a place to put his TV. Dales asks Mulder if love (not romantic love, but a true passion for something) can make a man shape shift, change him from a man into something else. He also tells Mulder that he needs to stop looking for the heart of the mystery and instead for the mystery of the heart. Later Mulder finally gets it–at least for this episode, as is usual he forgets the message fairly quickly. He invites Scully to play baseball–which is a metaphor for *his* real passion (the restoration of his lost family) that has the power to transform. He tells Scully that when they're focusing on the ball that their everyday concerns (which includes the conspiracy by the way) will fade away.

What actually changes Exley? He is still an alien up until he does the human thing which is to play a final game. He tells Dales that for his people, family comes first; which may be why sacrificing one's children is never going to gain points with the divine, no matter what it is in the name of. While the aliens may need to learn how to love from mankind, mankind may need to learn the importance of family from them. Exley tells the alien bounty hunter that his coming to play the final game is the right thing to do and the bounty hunter tells him that he jeopardizes the entire project by doing so. Mulder's quest is in many ways synonymous with the Project; both are sought to the exclusion of all else, but neither is the true path to getting home.

Is there metaphorical significance in the fact that this bounty hunter disguises himself as a member of the KKK? He seems to be part of the alien faction referenced in "End Game" that wants to maintain racial purity which would make him a Rebel. Exley later tells Arthur that the aliens just want to keep the two races separate–each should keep to their own much like segregation. Dales tells Mulder that all of the great baseball players are aliens, at least until they step on the diamond; all of the truly great never fit in with *anyone*– human or alien. Given that the words in the song that seem to be important are: *"We'll all be together in that land"* and *"I have a brother/sister in that land"* and *"Come with me to where I'm bound"* it would seem that both the fallen aliens (the Rebels and the Colonists) and humans can only find true paradise (home) *together* and not apart; the symbiosis that William represents.

FIELD TRIP

While not a mytharc episode, probably the most striking thing about "Field Trip" is it's similarities to it. The mushroom's acidic goo looks almost exactly like the aliens' green blood. In "Field Trip" as in the mytharc quest, Mulder and Scully are in a stupor and not seeing what's really happening.

Wallace and Angela Schiff are–like many monster of the week couples on the show– symbolic parallels for Mulder and Scully. Angela is angry at Wallace because he makes her chase him around the woods all day; he on the other hand is just basically clueless about her discomfort because he's so excited about what he's doing.

Later after Mulder finds him, Wallace becomes a pure projection of Mulder's own terror over Scully's abduction. Angela becomes a projection of Scully right down to having the exact same experience during her abduction as Scully does during hers. Interestingly, in "Field Trip" the hallucinating Mulder has the same reaction to the arrival of the aliens as he does in "Requiem"; he sets himself up for abduction which illustrates Mulder's desire to be taken. There is a replay of the brick wall theme from "How the Ghosts Stole Christmas" in Mulder's inability to see the way out of the cave until Wallace points it out to him. Wallace tells Mulder that the aliens are messing with his (Mulder's) mind. Angela and Wallace tell Mulder that the skeletons were decoys left there so that Mulder wouldn't know the truth and that the aliens are always watching.

Another interesting parallel is the location of Brown Mountain; it is in North Carolina, the same state where Mulder is later buried in "DeadAlive." Mulder's supposed death is a large part of Scully's hallucination. Does this reinforce how much she fears that eventuality especially in connection with the aliens? In Scully's hallucination, everyone else believes that Mulder is murdered in a ritualistic killing and skeletonized by acid or boiling. They are parroting her initial thoughts exactly. Instead of reveling in everyone's agreement–the approval she normally seeks– she's appalled that they are looking no further. Here is an important peek inside Scully's mind and motivations; she's a lot more willing to look beyond the most simple and logical explanation than she lets on. Instead she realizes that her role is to attempt to poke holes in Mulder's theories and that belief is borne out in this episode.

Mulder and Scully become trapped because they can no longer recognize what is real from what is hallucination; this is an important metaphor for their mytharc inability to tell the same and its destructiveness. At the end of "The Truth" Mulder and Scully are in exactly the same position on the motel bed as the Schiff's are in "Field Trip," right down to the position of Mulder's leg– which seems highly coincidental if it is not intentional. Instead of waking up to the real truth, they are still in their hallucination that Mulder's quest is righteous and it is slowly destroying them.

"Field Trip" is also intended to illustrate the importance of the dialectic nature of Mulder and Scully's partnership. Mulder's address of Hegal Place– for the philosopher Hegel – is probably not a coincidence; misspelling aside. Mulder's apartment is where two important discussions take place. The first is when Scully finds Mulder there with the Schiffs and the little Gray; this discussion is notable because it isn't dialectic. It is completely one-sided. After seeing and speaking with the little alien that Mulder abducts Scully becomes a complete believer even going so far as to dismiss evidence (the skeletons and the goo). Mulder can't believe she's buying it, which tells us something important about Mulder's mind and motivations. Apparently he realizes that some of the stuff he spouts is unbelievable and he expects and needs Scully to rein him in, even though he may complain about it. It isn't until the second discussion at Mulder's apartment–this time a dialectic one– that Scully begins to put the pieces together about what's really happening. During this dialogue Scully keeps pointing out the logic while Mulder keeps saying *"what can I say, I'm here."* Their positions are reversed later in Skinner's office, which ultimately leads to their real rescue. They have to work from both sides to the middle ground which is where the truth really lies.

Unfortunately they don't ultimately do this in the mytharc. Instead Mulder succeeds in getting Scully to believe–just like he does in "Field Trip" with the little Gray. But just like in

"Field Trip" this isn't the truth, at least not completely and in the most important ways; the dialectic nature of their partnership has been destroyed.

BIOGENESIS

"From space, it seems an abstraction — a magician's trick on a darkened stage. And from this distance one might never imagine that it is alive. It first appeared in the sea almost four billion years ago in the form of single-celled life. In an explosion of life spanning millions of years, nature's first multicellular organisms began to multiply... and then it stopped. 440 million years ago, a great mass extinction would kill off nearly every species on the planet leaving the vast oceans decimated and empty. Slowly, plants began to evolve,

then insects, only to be wiped out in the second great mass extinction upon the Earth. The cycle repeated again and again. Reptiles emerging, independent of the sea only to be killed off. Then dinosaurs, struggling to life along with the first birds, fish, and flowering plants — their decimations Earth's fourth and fifth great extinctions. Only 100,000 years ago, Homosapiens appear — man. From cave paintings to the Bible to Columbus and Apollo 11, we have been a tireless force upon the earth and off cataloguing the natural world as it unfolds to us. Rising to a world population of over five billion people all descended from that original single cell, that first spark of life. But for all our knowledge, what no one can say for certain, is what or who ignited that original spark. Is there a plan, a purpose or a reason to our existence? Will we pass, as those before us, into oblivion, into the sixth extinction that scientists warn is already in progress? Or will the mystery be revealed through a sign, a symbol, a revelation?"

The episode "Biogenesis" is about an artifact found in Africa in The Ivory Coast and its effect on Mulder. The writing on the rubbing is Cree (phonic Navajo) and includes Bible verses and the map of the human genome. The artifact acts as a catalyst for Mulder's brush with divinity. It reacts to the Bible in Dr. Merkmallen's office and marks the passage Genesis 1:28:

"And God blessed them, and God said unto them, Be fruitful, and multiply, and replenish the earth, and subdue it: and have dominion over the fish of the sea, and over the fowl of the air, and over every living thing that moveth upon the earth."

Not only is this a good description of mankind but the alien virus too.

There is the suggestion that the virus is an example of Panspermia. It seems likely since the meteor fragments seen in "Tunguska" are extraterrestrial and possibly from Mars. The interesting thing here is that Mars is a very cold place to be and the Grays do not develop without heat and more importantly the virus becomes inactive at cold temperatures. Perhaps this is the reason for the virus' original migration to Earth eons ago. The artifact emits Cosmic Galactic Radiation, which only occurs outside of our solar system which implies that the artifacts (and the ship) are originally from way out in space or instead another universe or a divine realm like Heaven or Samantha's starlight. The artifact also begins spinning in Albert Hosteen's hospital room. Perhaps it is the same material as the spinning vertebrae in "Existence" and could be indicative of Albert's role as a spirit guide or his connection to the divine.

It's likely that the virus Mulder harbors from his infection in "Tunguska" is reacting to the message and not to the medium. We know that the virus typically attaches itself to the pineal gland. It is widely held by those who believe in such things that the pineal gland is the seat of paranormal capabilities. If the virus, once activated, could somehow interact with Mulder's pineal gland, it may explain his sudden ability to hear thoughts. There is also the magic square concept that is intended for Mulder alone; an idea that makes sense if Mulder is predestined to be the father of William.

Krycek as the shadow is using the nanobot threat to force Skinner to spy on Mulder and Scully. Through his new powers Mulder realizes that Skinner has been compromised and understands his actions.

Scully travels to Africa to find out more about the artifact and finds the half-submerged spacecraft. The spaceships appear to act like a holy ark of some kind. They contain enormous power and the surface is covered with knowledge. Clearly they are connected to the mythic divine.

Diana is up to her old tricks of betrayal and is attempting to seduce Mulder yet again; this time physically. She also attempts to undermine Scully's trust in Mulder. Mulder does know when Scully shows up at the hospital and starts screaming for her. Presumably he has *finally* figured out that Diana is up to no good.

THE 6TH EXTINCTION

"I came in search of something I did not believe existed. I've stayed on now, in spite of myself. In spite of everything I've ever held to be true. I will continue here as long as I can... as long as you are beset by the haunting illness which I saw consume your beautiful mind. What is this discovery I've made? How can I reconcile what I see with what I know? I feel this was meant not for me to find but for you... to make sense of — make the connections which can't be ignored... connections which, for me, deny all logic and reason. What is this source of power I hold in my hand — this rubbing — a simple impression taken from the surface of the craft? I watched this rubbing take its undeniable hold on you, saw you succumb to its spiralling effect. Now I must work to uncover what your illness prevents you from finding. In the source of every illness lies its cure."

"The 6th Extinction" begins with Mulder hospitalized and in bad shape. His illness has caused never before seen activity in his temporal lobe which does not allow him to rest or sleep and causes fits of aggression. Perhaps this is the same mechanism that allows the super soldiers to go without sleeping. Mulder is apparently still in control to some degree since he feigns an attack on Skinner in order to slip him a note that asks him for help. In response, Skinner finds Michael Kritschgau who Mulder asks for personally. Perhaps in Scully's absence Mulder is looking for another disbeliever to help him figure out what's happening to him. Kritschgau runs a remote viewing test and discovers that not only is Mulder telepathic, but can also see into the future.

Meanwhile in Africa, Scully meets Dr. Amina Ngebe who assists her in translating the writing on the alien ship. In a reference to the Judeo/Christian mythology that this episode arc abounds with; when Dr. Barnes shows up the sea around the ship turns to blood and Scully is visited by a plague of insects at the appearance of a mysterious shaman. He appears to Scully at different times accompanied by various Biblical signs and appears to be a spirit guide. He ultimately tells her that this truth is not for her and touches her forehead approximately where her cancer lies. Maybe this touch is what makes her whole again and able to conceive. Scully is willing to now throw everything that she previously believed out the window in an effort to find a cure for Mulder. It is her first major crossroad, just as Mulder must face his in "Amor Fati."

Back at the hospital Diana tells Mulder that she knows what's happening to him. She tells him that she loves him and won't let him die. That she realizes that he now knows she has loyalties to Cigarette-Smoking Man, but that she has her reasons–although these remain unknown to the viewer, presumably Mulder can read her mind. She says that now they can be together, suggesting that something has now happened to open that path for them. Perhaps she is referring to Mulder's transfiguration.

In contrast, Scully asks Mulder to hang on because she thinks she has found the key to every question that has ever been asked. There is a big difference in the two bedside speeches from Diana and Scully–and the thoughts and emotions that Mulder can presumably pick up. Scully just wants Mulder to hang on and find his truth–her concern is not self-serving at all. Diana, on the other hand, is only truly interested in her own agenda and uses a proclamation of love as a means of manipulation.

THE 6TH EXTINCTION - AMOR FATI

"Amor Fati" is a huge allegory. The dream represents Mulder's search for the truth and that which would steer him from his fate. In Mulder's dream Cigarette-Smoking Man handcuffs him. Diana removes the obvious cuffs, but she put new ones on him that bind him just as tightly. She traps him with sex and an easy life of creature comforts in suburbia as long as he remains passive and plays by CSM 's rules. If Mulder's dream represents the path he does not take back when he still had a chance then this may be an indication that he does ultimately recognize the original intent of Diana 's role in his life. In his dream, she's meant to pacify him and to establish his connection with CSM. She ultimately takes him away from his real destiny by pacifying him. When Mulder continues to resist, Diana takes him to CSM 's house so that CSM can allay his fears about what Mulder has left undone. There he sees the "Redux II" fake Samantha–which he already *knows* is a fake, a fact he seems to conveniently forget about in the dream–just as he seems to ignore Diana 's real life betrayal.

The people who populate his dream are all those who have betrayed him in some way— Deep Throat, Diana, the fake Samantha, and CSM. They all act caring and nurturing, but their real goal is to keep him from realizing his destiny. Everyone seems intent on telling Mulder that he has no importance in the grand scheme of things. It is a huge lie and no doubt the main message of the dream–they want him to give up, but they realize that unless he believes his involvement will have no consequence he won't do it.

CSM tells Mulder in the dream that he can't contact Scully without endangering her. The people in the dream always refer to Scully as some kind of obligation or source of guilt–she's repeatedly put into a negative light, even going so far as to say that returning to her would mean Mulder's imminent death. The irony here is that not returning to her is the real road to his dying.

In the dream within a dream, Mulder meets a small boy on a beach; this is where Mulder is truly happy and at peace, not in the fantasyland being spun for him by CSM and Diana. However, as soon as Mulder begins buying into the lie the boy on the beach switches gears and starts to cry. As Mulder abandons his destiny (and his life) he is also abandoning the boy since William would never be born.

The boy on the beach represents Mulder's self or that which Diana as the personification of his anima calls childish, his drive for the truth. It is this that he would have to sacrifice in order to be with Diana in the manner in which he desires to be. He has already come to the realization that Diana is not an appropriate work partner so he has no real desire to pursue that avenue with her. However, she *does* represent his romantic aspirations and his Self is attempting to tell him that he can not have both pursuits. He has to choose between the truth and his desire for the seductiveness of Diana.

As the anima, when Diana calls Mulder's quest for the truth childish she is pointing out to him that his original quest is not the right one and that his real truth will only become manifest when he puts his feet down in the real world (which means putting what she represents aside) and become a father. Here is Mulder's feminine aspect of prophetic hunch and feelings doing what it is intended to do or the manifestation of the positive side of the archetype.

The dream speeds up even more and Mulder and Diana are married and have two boys, though neither are the special child that Mulder is fated to father. She dies sometime later still looking the same. CSM also looks the same later on whereas Mulder has aged. Her death may be a reference to the fact that the Diana Mulder thought he knew is dead to him and his aging may be a sign that he is dying. The two boys are never seen or mentioned again–even on Mulder's deathbed–interesting, since fatherhood is supposed to be his big joy.

In the dream, CSM tells Mulder that he knows about the boy and that it is a place born of memory and desire which likely means that Mulder's *real* desire is this child and that somewhere in his memory he knows this. During this sequence with the boy, he watches him destroy the UFO that he has built from the sand. The boy tells Mulder that he is the one destroying it and that he (Mulder) is supposed to help him (the boy). Possibly more clues to William and Mulder's role.

The boy (in CSM 's voice) tells Mulder that; *"The child is father to the man."* Perhaps from a mythological standpoint this child as William can be seen as Mulder's rebirth–the resolution of his quest and the start of his life beyond the realization of his destiny. All mythological heroes undergo a rebirth of some kind–this is usually the result of the hero coming to the realization that the truth he finds is not the same truth he began his journey searching for. It's possible that by the end of "Amor Fati" Mulder has begun to understand that the real truth isn't about proving the existence of aliens at all, but something far larger and he consequently undergoes a rebirth of a sort. His dreams of the boy on the beach may be what lead him to this conclusion. It could also refer to the boy (or in this case Mulder's self) acting as the Jungian father archetype.

Finally the apocalyptic scene with the aliens destroying the earth in fire isn't at all what Colonization is supposed to be about. The Colonists need the Earth whole and healthy in order to come home. However, in mythological terms, it does become the wasteland of the Grail myth when Mulder turns away from his destiny.

Back in the narrative's real world, CSM and Diana believe that he is Mulder's biological father–whether this is actually true or not is left ambiguous. CSM tells Diana that Mulder is a hero and his sacrifice will save mankind. However, whenever a sacrifice is demanded in *The X-Files* universe the end result doesn't work. Diana says that it would be nice to give Mulder a choice; this too is important because CSM never gives Mulder or Scully a choice in anything that happens to them. William 's conception on the other hand *is* their choice to make ("Per Manum" and "all things" both make a point of this) even if the method of his conception ends up surprising them.

Kritschgau tells Scully that Mulder's condition is caused by the rubbings reactivating the latent virus he is infected with in Tunguska. In the meantime Diana tries to blame Scully for what happens to Mulder, in turn; Scully appeals to Diana 's conscience and convinces her to help him. Here is yet another contrast between Diana and Scully, Diana seeks to passively blame, while Scully seeks to actively rescue. Albert Hosteen (or at least what looks like Albert Hosteen) appears to Scully in her apartment. He is acting as a spirit guide and tells her that she has to find Mulder before something happens to him, for the sake of *us* all and strongly suggests that the Walk-Ins and the other aliens have something riding on Mulder fulfilling his destiny too.

The second time Albert comes to Scully's apartment he tells her that she isn't looking in the right place and they pray. During this interlude Mulder's eyes to open during surgery and this seems to be the catalyst for Diana 's change of heart. Diana later slips Scully the *Native American Beliefs and Practices* book, which has a chapter on the apocalypse and the 6th extinction. Scully mentions that it contains a myth about a man who will save mankind although this may, in fact, be a reference to William and not Mulder.

Diana is murdered for giving Scully the means to save Mulder. However, it is important to note that she doesn't give Scully the key until *after* the damage has already been done. It is really no different than Well-Manicured Man's intervention on Scully's behalf in the movie. He may have given Mulder the means to find and vaccinate her, but it is Mulder that actually rescues her just as it is ultimately Scully that rescues him in "Amor Fati."

While on his deathbed at the end of his dream, Mulder has the strongest reaction to the news that Scully is dead. CSM keeps telling him to let go–he probably wants him to allow himself to die so that he can take over Mulder's destiny. As the king archetype, CSM isn't ready to abdicate in favor of Mulder. Fortunately Scully finally shows up and lets Mulder have it. She calls him a traitor, a deserter and a coward. She plays Judas' role from Martin Scorsese' the *Last Temptation of Christ* (the dream sequences are heavily based on it). She brings Mulder back from the brink of death so that he can fulfill his real destiny. She then leaves him which forces him to return to the real world to find her. When the real Scully shows up in the DoD room, the lies in the dream reveal themselves for what they really are– restraints.

One week later when Scully goes to see Mulder at his apartment he tells her that he was just coming to see her–she assumes he means he wants to work; this tells us a lot about where Scully still thinks she fits into his world. He is, in fact, coming to see her in order to tell her that Albert Hosteen has died the night before which means that his ghost couldn't have been at her apartment earlier it so it must have been a Walk-In using his persona.

Scully's lost and doesn't know what or who to believe anymore–her faith takes quite a beating in this arc. Mulder tells her that he was in the same place once referring to his dream and that he chose another life and fate and that in the end his world was upside down and unrecognizable. *She* is his one constant and that she's his friend and tells him the truth–the implication being that Diana didn't. The truth is verbally aligned with Scully here.

Mulder's last image of the boy on the beach implies that everything is again right in the world–possibly because he is now firmly on the correct path with the right partner. Importantly, together he and the boy *build* the spaceship not destroy it.

SEIN UND ZEIT

The "Sein Und Zeit"/ "Closure" arc is really confusing and doesn't tell us much about the mytharc except for some vague answers about what ultimately happens to Samantha. That aspect is what this analysis will focus on. The Walk-Ins make a personal appearance here and the fate of Samantha is revealed. Kathy Lee tells Mulder about the old souls (the Walk-Ins) that are looking for new homes–perhaps a reference to the desired transformed rebirth. In any case, they rescue Samantha from further tests by the Consortium and Cigarette-Smoking Man.

Mulder's mom commits suicide and she apparently wants to tell Mulder something before she dies. Perhaps the LaPierre case triggers her behavior or it is coincidental although it's a pretty big coincidence given what happens to both Samantha and Amber. Mulder's mother burns all her pictures of her children, perhaps a symbolic final destruction of the original family. Mulder can't make the final break from his old quest until he completely stops desperately clinging to his old broken and wounded family. His mother burns the pictures as a way of helping him let go.

Under protest Scully does the autopsy on Mulder's mom because Mulder believes the Consortium kills her. Instead Scully finds out that Teena was suffering from a terminal and disfiguring form of cancer and she believes this to be the reason Mrs. Mulder kills herself. Of course, cancer is a tool of the Consortium so perhaps they ultimately do kill her.

CLOSURE

"They said the birds refused to sing and the thermometer fell suddenly... as if God Himself had His breath stolen away. No one there dared speak aloud, as much in shame as in sorrow. They uncovered the bodies one by one. The eyes of the dead were closed as if waiting for permission to open them. Were they still dreaming of ice cream and monkey bars? Of birthday cake and no future but the afternoon? Or had their innocence been taken along with their lives, buried in the cold earth so long ago? These fates seemed too cruel, even for God to allow. Or are the tragic young born again when the world's not looking? I want to believe so badly; in a truth beyond our own, hidden and obscured from all but the most sensitive eyes... In the endless procession of souls, in what cannot and will not be destroyed. I want to believe we are unaware of God's eternal recompense and sadness. That we cannot see His truth. That that which is born still lives and cannot be buried in the cold earth. But only waits to be born again at God's behest... where in ancient starlight we lay, in repose."

Mulder doesn't sound like an atheist at all in the voiceover at the beginning of "Closure"–in fact, he sounds a lot like Scully; perhaps this is an illustration of the effect she has on him. Mulder wants his search for Samantha to be over even if that means finding her in a shallow grave somewhere the victim of a serial killer which illustrates just how much Mulder wants and needs to move on.

According to Harold Piller the Walk-Ins are good spirits that take children about to meet horrible fates that are never meant to be.

The little boy, another spirit guide, leads Mulder to Samantha 's diary and he finds out she lived with CSM, Cassandra and Jeffrey Spender until she ran away at age 14. She was subjected to tests and felt that the doctors have taken away her memories. She only had a vague memory of a brother who used to tease her. Scully finds a police report about Samantha and discovers that she had signs of self-abuse or more likely injuries from the tests on her body and was paranoid. She claimed she was being held hostage.

All of this appears to suggest that Mulder's memories of the night Samantha is taken are completely false or are manipulated in some way. Obviously someone took her and turned her over to CSM and the Project for the tests.

CSM is the one who calls off the search for Samantha in 1973. He's also apparently terminally ill by the events of "Closure" although it doesn't ultimately play out that way. He tells Scully that he has believed all along that Samantha is dead and that he hasn't told Mulder because there has been so much to protect–and that it is all gone now. He can't be referring to the Project because in "Per Manum" it's revealed that the efforts to create a hybrid or perfect soldier are still continuing. However, perhaps the super soldiers are now in control and not CSM. It's also possible that he thought Mulder no longer harbored the virus or brain function necessary for William's conception and he realizes that his own attempt at taking over that role has been unsuccessful. If this is the case, then something happens between "Closure" and "En Ami" to change his mind.

Perhaps the ghost of Mulder's mom finally answers his questions about Samantha while he sleeps. She must speak to his subconscious (not surprising in a story that owes a great deal to Jung) since he doesn't appear to remember any of it the next day.

Finally, he's led to the clearing by the little boy and is able to see Samantha one last time and finally say goodbye. He then tells Scully that he's now free, a vital step for Mulder to take in his journey. He feels that Samantha is dead and in a better place.

EN AMI

"En Ami" is another episode that makes a lot more sense when viewed in retrospect. On the surface it appears to be a con job by Cigarette-Smoking Man using the chips as bait. It is, sort of–but not necessarily for the reasons it appears. Again betrayal is a central theme; CSM 's betrayal of Scully and his assistant, the scientist's betrayal of the Project and Scully's unintentional betrayal of Mulder. Certainly Mulder doesn't like it when the shoe is on the other foot and he's the one ditched. Scully does try to get word to him that she is OK and to give him the information that is on the tape. However, true to form on *The X-Files*, since one of them is trying to work alone, it fails. Yet another reason why Mulder leaving and working alone in season nine is a mistake.

CSM engineers a scenario designed to spark Scully's interest and one she will be unable to resist pursuing. The chips do heal and they can apparently also keep someone alive for a lot longer than they would normally live. Scully is connected to immortality several times throughout the narrative and this is one more hint at it.

Presumably by this point CSM knows that Scully and Mulder attempt IVF and fail since the events of "Per Manum" appear to happen prior to the events in "En Ami." Given that *The X-Files* thrives on irony, it may be that CSM does do something to her chip in "En Ami" that is intended to correct her inability to conceive. It is unnecessary though because her fertility has already been restored via the divine in "The 6th Extinction" by either the shaman or the ship.

Somehow CSM knows that Scully's fertility has been returned–either due to the tests that are done during her IVF attempts or whatever he may have do with the chip while she is unconscious in "En Ami." In his attempts to steal Mulder's destiny CSM now has to get Scully alone and try to seduce her because he knows that conception via artificial means will not work. CSM protects Scully throughout the show because she has to live in order for William to happen.

In "En Ami", CSM is redeemed to some degree because he does want to save the world, however, in his hubris; he wants to be the one who does it–the archetypal conquering hero and on his terms. Here as in "Amor Fati," CSM just wants to be Mulder. For all his power, he's envious of and covets the one thing it can't give him–the kind of bond that exists between Scully and Mulder. No one has ever given him that. In fact, everyone turns against him in the end–including Diana Fowley. She is probably his attempt at the same kind of relationship that Mulder enjoys with Scully. Instead it is the antithesis of it; based on betrayal and lies instead of trust and the truth.

ALL THINGS

The main two points behind the episode "all things" are fate and choice. Daniel is Scully's Diana Fowley. Since she externalizes her masculine aspect versus her feminine he is a mirror and the physical manifestation of her ruling negative animus. In "all things" she comes to the same crossroad that Mulder does in "Amor Fati." She has to choose whether to follow the path that will give her over entirely to her animus–life with Daniel–or the one which will bring the two halves of the hero into balance. Again, it isn't that Scully has to forgo any hope for a normal life; it's that she has to choose to do so with the man that balances her, not the one who would drag her further into the darkness of emotional isolation. Daniel didn't want Scully to join the FBI when they were together–he has a controlling and patronizing attitude towards her. The implication is Scully joins the FBI as an excuse to leave him–or at least that's what he believes.

Another major theme in "all things" is that buried or repressed shame or guilt can cause illness and derail one's life. For her, following the wrong path with Daniel will lead to complete emotional repression and its inherent ills. In doing so she also forfeits becoming mother to William, the physical manifestation of the transformed hero. Perhaps this is a suggestion that until Scully fully lets go of her pent up negative feelings about what happened with Daniel, her infertility can't fully be reversed and it might explain why the earlier IVF treatments are not successful. The real underlying message here may be that feelings–negative or positive–have the power to transform. Once she does let go, she is able to consummate her relationship with Mulder and conceive William. Perhaps Mulder's comment about David Crosby is a reference to the IVF attempts. Otherwise it would be extremely insensitive. Instead it may be an indication that Mulder recognizes that Scully is asking more of him than to be just an "anonymous" sperm donor with no ties to the resulting child.

A Walk-In in the form of the blonde woman appears is spirit guide who is orchestrating the events that lead up to Scully's momentous decision. It's important to note that in the end it remains Scully's choice. She isn't forced into anything.

Scully's vision in the temple is her Annunciation. There are several parallels between William and the Christian myth's conception and birth of the Christ. Mulder is pictured several times in her vision–all scenes of events important to her. Everyone else only gets one shot.

In "all things" Scully comes to the realization that she is no longer the same person that she once was. She also realizes that there is only one right path and that hers is with Mulder regardless of whether he can or will give her a normal life. Mulder thinks that says a lot, a lot, a lot and so it does.

JE SOUHAITE

The monster of the week episode "Je Souhaite" makes some pretty good points mytharcwise. *The X-Files* mythology is almost an anti-hero's journey in a way. The road of sacrifice and one heroic man grand quest against evil doesn't pan out at all and the genie and Scully in "Je Souhaite" explain why. The genie points out how no religion on Earth has ever been able to change every person's heart to pure good and that Mulder's desire to do so is extremely egotistical. Scully tells Mulder that the process of achieving a perfect world is mankind's purpose and how dangerous it is for one man to try to circumvent it.

Leslie and Anton Stokes never see the obvious wish, getting Leslie out of the wheelchair even though the genie tries to point it out. At least they don't until Leslie figures it out one second before being blown to bits. Mulder never quite sees the obvious either no matter how often the divine tries to tell him. In his case he could escape his emotional wheelchair if he'd only recognize that he can, instead he appears to want to immortalize it in pure gold like Leslie does.

When Mulder asks the genie what she would wish for she basically tells him that she would wish to be happy with the life she has instead of worrying about the life she doesn't, to merely sit down with a great cup of coffee and watch the world go by. This is probably an important point for Mulder given his earlier dream of the perfect life in the seventh season episode "Amor Fati" and his perhaps lingering disappointment that he isn't going to get it. Or even possibly his overwhelming desire to find some all-important truth that can save the world, even though it may not be his destiny to do so. In the end, when he invites Scully over for the movie and popcorn, he's attempting to be happy with the life he has (hence his comment that it seems like the right thing to do), unfortunately it's right before he's abducted in "Requiem" and he apparently forgets the lesson by the time he gets back.

In a way, it's sad that Scully continues to represent a life that he has to learn to accept instead of being a part of the life he wishes he had or would find perfect. Maybe this inability to see Scully's true importance is the real reason Mulder ultimately fails to be transformed. Until he can understand and appreciate the difference between Eros and true platonic Love, he will continue to desire the lesser of the two and fail to value the real truth.

Finally, Mulder thinks the genie is evil because bad things happen to folks who come into contact with her. She isn't the real problem though. It's mankind's greed that does them in; an apt metaphor for the aliens and the Consortium. The correct wish is the one that frees her and returns her humanity. It is again, a metaphor for the idea that the real answer to the possible extinction of mankind (or the bad result from the greedy wish of conquering the aliens and stealing their technology) would be to free the aliens, not to keep them enslaved so that they can continue to grant wishes.

REQUIEM

"Requiem" takes us full circle back to Billy Miles and Bellefleur Oregon. The abysmally bad alien pilots strike again and collide with a military plane. Oddly, the forest is on fire where the ship is but then appears healed later. The old "X" in the road that Mulder spray paints in the pilot episode still marks the spot for anomalous electrical disturbances. Perhaps this is one of the light houses or areas with access to the Origin Place or the divine.

The theme of "Requiem" seems to be Mulder's realization that maybe it's time to get out of the car. In a typical bout of Mulder's bad luck and timing, he finally finds the aliens and is abducted just when he's prepared to walk away. However, since this abduction ultimately cures him of a terminal brain illness, maybe it is not such bad luck after all. In addition, it is possible that Scully's pregnancy is the catalyst for the abductions in the first place. If these are the Walk-Ins then they may be trying to put everything right at least from their point of view before William's birth.

Scully certainly seems different in "Requiem"; she defends Mulder's work and his beliefs, and actively encourages him to forget about the audit and go to Oregon. She even seems to be enjoying herself. Just as Scully has started to really get into things, Mulder has decided to step back.

Mulder's reaction to seeing Scully with Theresa's baby makes a lot more sense and is more poignant after the events of "Per Manum" and the knowledge that they have been trying to conceive via IVF. Apparently Theresa Hoese isn't barren like Scully was. Theresa makes a comment that may be enlightening when she tells Mulder and Scully that her husband Ray's abductions were much more terrifying than hers. Perhaps they were abducted by either different factions or one by aliens and the other by the Consortium. In any case, they both apparently have what the aliens are looking for in "Requiem" as does Mulder; the brain anomalies seen in the "Biogenesis" arc.

Since the bounty hunter ignores Theresa's baby he/she is not likely to be special or alien in any way which indicates that together Theresa and Ray do not have the same qualities that Mulder and Scully do and can't create the messianic child. The Hoese baby does appear to be immune to the retrovirus in the green blood so gaining immunity must not be the deciding factor. In fact, that immunity may be the very reason why this child is not the one.

The scene in Skinner's office is a recreation of Da Vinci's *Last Supper*. There are two important pieces of information here. Skinner is standing in Peter's spot and Scully is in Judas'; this doesn't mean that Scully actively betrays Mulder. It does mean that she plays as pivotal and necessary role in his abduction just as Judas plays in Jesus ' crucifixion. Of all the apostles, only Judas directly affects Jesus' fate–one that could not be ultimately realized without his participation.

Marita and Krycek return. Marita appears to have recovered from her bout with the alien virus and tests. She's working for Cigarette-Smoking Man who appears to be on his last legs, but don't count the king out just yet. She springs Krycek from a Tunisian prison where

he is thrown for attempting to sell something of CSM 's–probably the information from Kritschgau's laptop, which he steals in "Amor Fati."

CSM sounds desperate to find the ship and he seems to already know that folks are being abducted. Somehow CSM always seems to know what the aliens are up to. He believes that by possessing this particular ship will give him the answers to every imaginable question and an opportunity to rebuild the Project. Since the super soldier project is still going strong based on later episodes, what exactly does he want to rebuild and what is it about this ship that he's looking for? The Consortium have had ships in the past so it can't be that alone, unless it's the timing of this particular access or this ship belongs to a faction that the Consortium has not had direct contact with before, like the Walk-Ins.

12

THE EPISODES – SEASON EIGHT

WITHIN

"Within" begins Scully's dream invoking strong birth imagery of the am-
niotic sack and fluid. It's actually Mulder in the ship being disconnected from
the same kind of tube that Scully has in the ship in the movie. Scully continues
to have dreams about what is happening to Mulder throughout this arc using the
same connection they had during her abduction in "Ascension."

Kersh is promoted to Deputy Director and is now Skinner's boss too. He's
still the same bastard he was before. He tells Scully and Skinner that if they
mention aliens they will lose their jobs. He represents rejection of the divine.
Kersh makes veiled comments about instincts and flying by the seat of his
pants–a Mulderish trait and dangerous one at that. In contrast, Doggett is more
like Scully and thinks things through. Based on Kersh 's later affiliations, he is
probably working for the super soldiers at this point; however, he does not
appear to be one himself.

Special Agent John Doggett is heading up the FBI manhunt to find Mulder.
It appears as though Scully and Skinner are considered suspects of some kind.
Skinner wants to tell the truth about what happened, however, Scully doesn't
want him to lose his job. As a result, Skinner as the Peter figure, denies Mulder.

Doggett insinuates that Mulder was confiding in various women at the
Bureau, that he didn't trust Scully and found her to be too ambitious. Scully
doesn't buy it and discovers Doggett's deception and his intent to pump her for
information. The writers choose to use these two specific accusations because
both go completely against Mulder's known characterization. While he may be
vulnerable to a specific kind of woman, he most certainly does not casually

sleep around and it's highly unlikely that he would tell these conquests that he doesn't trust Scully. The only narrative value of Doggett's comments is to illustrate his motive, which is to see if Scully has information that she is not coming forward with. Apparently the trust between Mulder and Scully is well known since it's the first thing everyone attempts to attack when trying to divide them. On the other hand, Mulder apparently *doesn't* tell Scully about his illness and approaching death so he was still hiding things from her.

Doggett catches Scully asleep in Mulder's bed and most likely draws a few conclusions from it. Scully doesn't exactly set him straight, although she does try to pawn it off as feeding the fish. She is not overly concerned about Doggett's assumptions or she may be just unwilling to lie about her and Mulder's relationship when confronted. She doesn't deny Mulder.

Doggett already knows where the fish food is which reveals that he has already searched Mulder's apartment. He shows up looking to find out more about Mulder's trips to Raleigh, North Carolina.

In the meantime, Mulder is apparently being tortured on some kind of evil looking chair and it is very reminiscent of another crucifixion. He has the nails through the hands and feet (wrists and ankles anyway, which is technically more accurate), the crown of thorns in the hooks in his face and the cut in his side with the vivisection; yet another death and rebirth on the hero's journey. While this looks and probably is horrific, it doesn't mean that it is evil. Remember Mulder and possibly the other abductees are dying from a terminal brain illness that is not diagnosable and is untreatable. As Jeremiah Smith tells Scully later, he's trying to save the abductees so these procedures may be necessary to do so. In the Christian myth, Jesus also goes through a horrific death in order to rise again into the divine.

Mulder also has a hole drilled into his soft palate–probably to get at his pineal gland. Obviously the aliens have either never discovered anesthesia– perhaps they don't feel pain and assume humans don't either–or they just don't care if they cause the subject pain. One other possibility is that Mulder isn't actually feeling any pain; instead he's reacting to his terror over what they are doing to him.

The Lone Gunmen find data that suggests that the ship that took Mulder is in the Arizona desert echoing the barren desert theme from the Grail mythology since the world has not yet been healed. While Skinner and Scully are at the gas station she sees the cloaked ship– although she apparently doesn't realize what she's looking at. The Flemingtown School for the Deaf (which may be a reference to Sir Alexander Fleming who won the Nobel Prize in physiology or medicine in 1945 and was a pioneer in vaccination) is 20 minutes away or approximately 20 miles. She later walks to the ship from the school so it has to move closer to the school at some point after they stop for gas.

The alien bounty hunter disguised as Mulder steals Scully's computer. In addition to her notes on the spacecraft in Africa, Scully has a great deal of information stored on it from the book that she receives from Diana Fowley during Mulder's illness in "Amor Fati." Since Mulder's brain illness seems to be a major factor in his abduction–it makes sense that the aliens would want all the information on it that they can get or perhaps they are doing just what Scully suspects them of and destroying all evidence of their existence. The Walk-Ins are apparently also looking for Gibson Praise. They do apparently have some idea that he is in the Southwest and slowly narrow it down to the school.

There are a lot of timing inconsistencies in the eighth and ninth seasons. Based on information from "The Gift" Mulder is abducted in mid-May. However, Doggett also has car rental receipts from four consecutive weekends in that month and oddly it is still mid-May in "Within." More time line inconsistency surrounds Mulder's illness. Doggett says that the events of the "Biogenesis" arc happened a year ago, which would put them around May 1999. That's odd, since a week after his impromptu brain surgery and rescue Mulder is wearing a Yankees victory cap which suggests that his and Scully's meeting is post World Series. It's a minor detail that can easily be overlooked and it should now be assumed that his brain surgery happens in May.

WITHOUT

"We live in a darkness of our own making; blind by a habitant world all but unseen by us. A world of beings traveling through time and space; imaginable to us only as flights of fancy. Who are these beings we dare to imagine but fear to accept? What dark work goes on inside their impossible machines cloaked from us by invisible forces? If they can know our secrets, why can't we know theirs?"

As they generally do Scully's voice over at the beginning of "Without" sheds a bit more light on the myth. The darkness is of mankind's making *not* the aliens and our inability to accept them is born out of fear.

An alien bounty hunter, disguised as Mulder, tries to abduct Gibson. He is pretty quiet – he is, in fact, not very good at impersonating folks at all until his later attempt at the hospital as Skinner. It is a fairly pronounced difference, so it may be intended to distinguish between two separate bounty hunters. In any case, his behavior with Doggett and Gibson is decidedly odd.

Apparently a bounty hunter can take a licking and keep on ticking or at least this one can. He jumps off the cliff and gets back up with nothing more than what appears to be a broken arm. He snaps the arm back into place, which lends more proof to the theory that these aren't really bodies as we know them. Is this death-defying stunt intended to show Doggett that he isn't Mulder, or human for that matter? Otherwise it makes no sense for him to do something quite this extreme, he could have easily allowed Doggett to just shoot him and disable Doggett with the toxic gas. He lets Gibson get away fairly easily too. Either he's just an incompetent one or he's not really trying to do what it appears he is.

Gibson isn't able to heal himself. He breaks his leg running away and the injury remains. He also bleeds red, something already established in "The Beginning." While he doesn't appear to be infected with the virus he does have alien DNA–or more correctly certain genes are turned on. He isn't, however, like William. It appears that William is able to heal to some degree based on the fact that Scully doesn't miscarriage even though she's put through the wringer a few times during her pregnancy.

Gibson has a similar connection to Mulder that Scully does–he also dreams about what's happening to Mulder on the ship and can feel him nearby. He tells Scully that she is now so close. Mulder also knows when Scully comes within a few feet of the ship and calls out to her before she heads off to the hospital to protect Gibson.

Skinner believes that Kersh is the one who gives Doggett the files on Gibson and that Doggett is being set up to fail. In order for this to work, Kersh has to know what's really going on. If he is working for the super soldiers, then they have a stake in the outcome too.

A gun shot to the back of the neck kills the bounty hunter or at least the one impersonating Skinner. In the past it hasn't been enough–the ice pick didn't even work in "Herrenvolk." Perhaps this bounty hunter is never intended to succeed or is fundamentally different than the other ones. They do all appear to have identical bodies just like the Gregors. Scully recognizes the alien bounty hunter and finally believes that he is an alien. The bounty hunter also takes a pretty big chance of harming William and throws Scully across the room, but he does not kill her as he could easily do. She and Gibson also don't have the burns from the toxic green blood.

By the end of "Without" Mulder appears to be dead; he's no longer conscious in any case and a group of the bounty hunters stand around him.

PER MANUM

In "Per Manum" it is revealed that Scully really wants a baby and she wants it to be genetically hers (and Mulder's) as well. Mulder still has the vial of Scully's ova that he steals in "Memento Mori." He had the ova tested at one time and finds out that they are no longer viable. He hasn't told her about them because he didn't want to hurt her during the time she was dying of cancer. He doesn't give any reason for withholding the information after that. Mulder is willing to father Scully's child via IVF provided it does not come between them. They attempt IVF at least once and it fails. Scully has no more chances to conceive in this way.

There is awkwardness between them in the scene where Mulder says yes. It appears to be gone by the time she later tells him the procedure fails. Mulder is much more comfortable in her apartment and with her in the later scene. He's sleeping on her couch and appears to have made himself at home, whereas in the earlier scene he is very much a guest.

It is later revealed in "Essence" that the Project doctors are trying to gestate alien babies in order to harvest their stem cells. These babies who appear to be Grays die soon after birth. The alien embryos are apparently implanted in women without their consent and the Project doctors are willing to kill the mothers in order to avoid exposure.

Scully's OB, Dr. Parenti has a connection to the doctors at Zeus Genetics who are producing alien and deformed human babies. Since the Project is attempting to produce super soldiers, Scully is a prime candidate given her prior genetic profile and manipulation. For some reason however, they don't choose to use her for this like they do Mary Hendershot. There must be some reason for this given that it is a prime opportunity.

Obviously the Project doctors don't want Scully pregnant–if they had; the IVF would not have failed, at the very least she would be pregnant with an alien baby. Dr. Parenti goes through the motions, probably to make sure she doesn't go somewhere else to try. If there was any chance of the ova being viable the last thing the doctors would want is for Scully, out of desperation, to take them to some other fertility clinic and risk the chance that the procedure would work, especially if the ova have been tampered with. So Parenti tells her that it might work and goes through the motions. If the ova aren't, in fact, viable–or they don't want her to think they are–it's doubtful that the procedure would ever make it as far as implantation. IVF doctors implant *embryos* not *ova*. If they didn't want Scully pregnant they most certainly would not implant viable embryos and take the chance that the procedure would succeed. It is likely Dr. Parenti tells her that the fertilization procedure fails on all the ova and leaves it at that. The Project doctors must have gotten a big surprise when she later turns up pregnant anyway.

Since Parenti is her doctor he would know that she believes it to be by natural means– although she may not tell him who the presumed daddy is. Since he does know who she uses as a donor, he probably at least suspects the baby's real paternity. Given Scully's genetic profile, they are sure to be very interested in her child, especially if they have any inkling of the prophecy. Since this is a super soldier operation and it is clear in later in "Essence" and "Existence" that they suspect that Scully's baby is special, it is very likely that they do.

At this point the Project doctors want not only access to Mary Hendershot's baby and she's looking like she's going to run, but also need as much knowledge as they can get on Scully's. She's already had complications prior to her 14-week point so as a doctor she's unlikely to agree to an amniocentesis without an extremely good reason and the Project doctors need that data.. If she's carrying a normal child then they don't really care. On the other hand, if she's carrying the prophesized special child they most certainly would want to know.

So up steps Duffy Haskell with a story that matches hers exactly–right down to their alien baby being implanted in their bedroom. If the doctors think she conceived via IVF, they would use that as Duffy's wife's suspected conception method. Mary Hendershot story is just another nail in the coffin so they allow her to go to Scully, which induces even more fear and paranoia. It also explains why it's so easy for Scully to get into the lab with the deformed fetuses and why the tape is so obviously faked.

William is *The X-Files* myth's version of the virgin birth a staple for the hero archetype. That's not to say that Scully and Mulder did not conceive William naturally; but that Scully is barren. For the narrative to imply William's true genesis, all other viable options have to first be discredited, including assisted conception. "Per Manum" also allow the writers to illustrate Mulder and Scully's mutual desire to have a child. In the grand scheme of things it's vital that William was ultimately the product of their choice and not someone else's.

Doggett finally finds out about Scully's pregnancy and is concerned for her well-being.

THIS IS NOT HAPPENING

Scully has been looking for Mulder all along–although she apparently isn't using the same methods that Richie has in his search for Gary. There is a marked contrast between Richie's reaction to finding Gary dead and Scully's with Mulder; the difference between good friend and lover.

The character of Monica Reyes is introduced. She apparently worked with Doggett on the search for his son. It's also strongly implied that Luke Doggett is found dead – something that is later confirmed in "Empedocles." Interestingly, she smokes Morley lights but is trying to stop. Smoking is normally a symbol of evil intent in this narrative; however, she doesn't fit the mold. In fact, she generally acts as a wise advisor or guide.

The aliens that abduct Mulder and the people from Oregon are dumping them near death in remote areas. However, according to Monica whoever is doing it appears to care about them. Jeremiah Smith is still out and about and he is healing the abductees as they are dropped off. It is the last of the Jeremiahs and he is always there when an abductee is dumped which suggests that he is working with the Walk-Ins and accomplishing something important in the grand scheme of things. He tells Cigarette-Smoking Man in "Talitha Cumi" that he no longer believes in the Project and hegemony so he is no longer a worker bee for the Consortium nor likely one for the Colonists. Instead he is now working to reintegrate the divine and mankind for the benefit of all by attempting to fulfill the prophecy.

He tells Scully that he's the only one and is working to save the abductees. There are two ways of interpreting what Jeremiah is doing at this point. The first is that he somehow knows where the Colonists are dropping off the abductees and rescues them from their fate as alien replicants. The second is that the alien ship that abducts and seemingly tortures the abductees is a Walk-In ship and they are trying to undo everything that has been done to the abductees previously *and* they need them to become witnesses (as alien replicants) at the time of William's birth. The latter is most likely the case. An important note to remember in this arc is that the Walk-Ins are not invaders at all so any reference to a coming alien invasion is likely to refer to either the Colonists or the super soldiers.

Jeremiah has an assistant named Absalom who appears to believe that he is doing God's work by healing the abductees. Mulder is found dead and has apparently been that way for a while. Jeremiah doesn't want the FBI to find him; he wants to help him but is interrupted. Jeremiah is taken by the Walk-Ins ship and is unable to heal Mulder. It's likely that what Jeremiah was really doing was helping the abductees go through the transformation in a quick and painless manner versus the one that Billy Miles has to go through. He is hastening the change not stopping it given that these abductees later show up at William's birth as alien replicants

Scully finally sees an alien spacecraft in all its glory and it is a round one like the one in Antarctica which is important as a circle is a symbol of the divine. In fact, it may *be* the same ship as the one in Antarctica. She also appears to have become a believer at some point. She's certainly pretty good at picking Jeremiah Smith out of the pack. She is devastated throughout "This Is Not Happening." She still has the psychic connection to Mulder and her tendency to see ghosts. She expects to find Mulder dead on some level and is trying to prepare herself for that eventuality–although when he is found she can't believe it. Maybe their connection, while weak, has not been completely severed since he isn't actually dead.

DEADALIVE

Scully tells Skinner that Mulder dies before his truth is fully revealed to him. Obviously she doesn't mean the existence of aliens because Mulder most certainly has gotten his answer to that question. Nor could it be the answer about Samantha since Mulder finds that in "Closure." This one little comment holds an important clue about the true nature of the truth. Whether Scully is consciously aware of it or it's just the writers' way of foreshadowing–she probably means William and the truth he embodies. Mulder dies before he knew the baby even exists and certainly before his son's real role is revealed and the family is briefly restored.

The treatment for exposure to the green blood is exactly the same in "End Game" and "Emily" as the one Scully uses to cure Mulder in "DeadAlive." Those exposed to the green blood carry a retrovirus which kills them by thickening the blood. Perhaps the virus (Purity) that Mulder is infected with and the retrovirus are one and the same; the different reactions are based on both methods of exposure, viral strain and mutation. The airborne version, or the retrovirus, is either a defense mechanism–albeit a fairly unsuccessful one–or the inadvertent result of the virus ' exposure to oxygen. Kresge, in "Emily", and presumably Skinner in "Without," are both cured the very same way, which means Mulder is not the only one who can respond to this treatment.

Mulder ultimately doesn't play the messianic role–while he is resurrected (reborn) in "DeadAlive," he does not transfigure to the divine in the end. That's not his destiny. William, on the other hand, is the one fundamentally transformed and united with the divine. Krycek as the shadow is out to destroy the creative and healing power (William). He fails, but Jeffrey Spender – out of fear – later accomplishes it in "William," not by killing him, but by destroying his divine nature or at least appearing to.

Skinner has become much stronger in his convictions since "Requiem." He no longer waffles around or sits on the fence. He makes the difficult choice that he would have avoided in the past.

Billy Miles tells Scully that the aliens are trying to save mankind. Again, another clue that he is taken by the Walk-Ins. He's behaving strangely enough that Scully picks up on the fact that he's no longer the same. Mulder is definitely Mulder again. His little *"who are you"* crack is probably meant to get back at her for her *"got you big time"* in the movie and to illustrate that he's who he's supposed to be unlike Billy Miles.

THREE WORDS

Mulder no longer has the brain illness that is killing him during the seventh season and he's healing quickly from his ordeal and is in perfect health; this is no doubt a residual effect of the viral infection. Here is the reason the abductees are taken to begin with. If the Walk-Ins have been trying to create the messianic child and if the brain illness or more likely whatever was causing it is a vital ingredient then once the child has been conceived, they can then cure all the abductees. They could just leave them all to die, but that's what the Consortium does, not them.

Mulder even still has his apartment and all his stuff; perhaps this is intended to illustrate that Scully never really gave up hope.

The genetic records revealed in "Herrenvolk" are now being kept electronically at the Census Bureau instead of the Social Security Administration or perhaps these files are a back up. In any case, this is basically the same data that had been in the files in the mine in "Paper Clip." Someone or something had been keeping records of who is genetically predisposed to being taken over by an alien or who would be a good match to become a super soldier. Mulder, Scully, Absalom, and Howard Salt all believe it to be the aliens, but since this is the work of the Project, it is far more likely to be for use in the super soldier program. Especially given that it is Knowle Rohrer who is later revealed to be a super soldier that sets Mulder and Doggett up.

The super soldiers want Mulder and Doggett dead. It is revealed in season nine that William's importance is some how linked to Mulder's presence in his life so they must want to forestall that. It suggests that while based on his actions in "Per Manum," Knowle Rohrer wants William born the super soldiers do *not* want Mulder to be a part of his son's life. William 's potential is the real target.

Howard Salt and Absalom 's knowledge of the coming invasion are also enough to get them killed, but it is not the aliens who do it, it's probably the super soldiers or at least those acting in their behalf. Fight the future is an important phrase here. It ties back to the movie and Strughold's comment that a single man can't fight the future which is again a human/Project tie not an alien one.

Scully feels that Doggett is above reproach even if Mulder doesn't yet trust him. Mulder begins to maneuver Doggett into becoming the heir-apparent of the x-files. With these subtle manipulations, he has unwittingly begins down the same path as CSM.

Scully has always been extremely sensitive to the fact that the x-files and Mulder's quest come first. Mulder is constantly accusing her of trying to interfere with that in "Three Words." She reacts by not using the baby's paternity as leverage even though she is desperate to keep him safe.

VIENEN

Vienen means *"they come,"* however, does it refer to the aliens or to the humans that are disturbing the black oil? According to Greek mythology, Orpheus is the greatest musician and poet. His wife Eurydice is killed by a serpent and he goes to the underworld to bring her back. Hades allows her return provided Orpheus does not look back until they are on the surface. He fails and Eurydice slips back to the underworld again.

The Galpex-Orpheus Oil Rig is receiving a broadband signal which is the catalyst for the events on the rig. Here it would appear that the aliens–most likely the Walk-Ins–are attempting to rescue the alien sentience in the black oil residing in the newly discovered field in the Gulf of Mexico. The signal is akin to the music that Orpheus sings to Hades in order to rescue Eurydice. In fear and misunderstanding, the two immune Huecha Indians along with Mulder and Doggett wreak havoc and the attempt fails and with the blowing of the rig, the black oil slips back to the underworld.

The virus does not infect hosts randomly and only appears to do so when it is absolutely necessary. It avoids infecting Mulder and Doggett until they figure out what is going on and become a threat. Even then it allows them to leave the rig before it is blown up. Mulder and Doggett are basically herded off of it when the helicopter shows up.

It sounds like this oil field shows up suddenly; perhaps all of the black oil now massing together in one place. If Mulder is correct in assuming that it is using the rig as a means of spreading infection, destroying the rig makes no sense.

Mulder apparently believes himself to be William's biological father otherwise the comment *"tell the kid I went out swinging"* has no real meaning. Given that Mulder willingly passes the torch to Doggett and walks away from the x-files. He appears to be choosing to put the baby and Scully first now that there is someone else to take over the search for the aliens. He certainly doesn't come across as all that broken up over it. In "Vienen" Mulder is playing more of a mentor role here and at no time suspects Doggett of being in on anything. Instead he is focused on getting Doggett to understand the threat.

ESSENCE

> *"We call it the miracle of life. Conception: A union of perfect opposites — essence transforming into existence — an act without which mankind would not exist and humanity cease to exist. Or is this just nostalgia now? An act of biology commandeered by modern science and technology? God-like, we extract, implant, inseminate... and we clone. But has our ingenuity rendered the miracle into a simple trick? In the artifice of replicating life can we become the creator? Then what of the soul? Can it, too, be replicated? Does it live in this matter we call DNA? Or is its placement the opposite of artifice, capable only by god. How did this child come to be? What set its heart beating? Is it the product of a union? Or the work of a divine hand? An answered prayer? A true miracle? Or is it a wonder of technology — the intervention of other hands? What do I tell this child about to be born? What do I tell Scully? And what do I tell myself?"*

In Mulder's opening voice over a basic concept of the truth is revealed; the artificial versus the natural genesis of life and origin of a new species. Is William the product of the former or the latter?

Billy Miles as a Walk-In alien replicant is destroying the artificial in the work of the Project and the doctors associated with it. Here he is playing the sane role as an avenging angel, hence the Biblical manner in which he speaks. He and presumably the Walk-Ins consider the resulting alien babies to be abominations. The Walk-Ins are destroying the work that leads to the super soldiers who are the real evil. Billy doesn't however kill Mulder when he has the chance although on the surface it appears like he will. Another narrative red herring by the writers intended to enforce the evil alien notion in both the viewers' and in Mulder's mind. Billy also destroys Duffy Haskell; so whatever he and Lizzy Gill are up to is against the Walk-Ins' agenda.

Lizzy tells Mulder, Doggett, Skinner, and Agent Crane (who is now secretly a super soldier) that the alien babies are being created in order to harvest stem cells for other experiments. According to Lizzy Scully's baby is a perfect human child with no human frailties and that William was *not* created in a lab.

Agent Crane sends Doggett on a wild goose chase after Billy Miles who is actually on his way to Scully's apartment. Mulder believes that Billy wants to kill Scully and William and is trying to get her to safety. Apparently Agent Crane believes the same thing and is trying to allow it to happen.

For some reason Krycek (who is working with the super soldiers) claims to want to protect Scully and William from Billy Miles and the alien replicants who he says want to kill them. He says that the aliens only now found out about William's true nature. He has to be lying here–no surprise, he always does–because the Walk-Ins not only know about William, but are the reason he's conceived in the first place. The important thing to remember is that Billy's true intentions with regards to Scully and William are never clear–everyone is simply assuming the worse just as they always do with the aliens.

Mulder is however, fully concentrating on protecting Scully and not on the x-files aspects of the events. Here he is acting as the good father.

EXISTENCE

The episode "Existence" would have marked the end of the successful hero's journey for Mulder and the myth. However, since he can't ultimately give up his original quest in season nine he ends up becoming the new wounded king in place of CSM and starts down the same destructive path.

Billy Miles as an alien replicant can reassemble himself even after horrific injury. He has a metal vertebra that can replicate itself back into a human made of flesh and blood–albeit a pretty indestructible one. The ships can self-repair and the artifact in the "Biogenesis" arc spun so it's probably a good bet there is some connection. Billy Miles is the product of alien technology through and through. The virus has used all kinds of mannequins to get around and this is probably just one more variant on the theme. Apparently the Walk-Ins already have the knowledge to achieve what the Colonists are working towards.

One important thing to note is that when Billy has murder on his mind he *quickly* dispatches his intended target. In both Mulder and Reyes case he only tosses them aside. He has plenty of opportunity to kill them if that is what he really wants to do. Perhaps he isn't doing what Krycek accuses him of and is attempting to protect Scully not harm her. The game warden may have shot Billy because she is still operating as a human. The one main difference between Billy and the others is that he seems to have lost his humanness entirely. Maybe that's what Jeremiah is able to help the other abductees keep.

Jeremiah Smith must *not* destroy the virus when he heals the returning abductees because they all show up to witness William 's birth and appear to be under some kind of alien control. Given this and the Biblical imagery in this episode, this may be an indication that the replicants are associated with the Walk-Ins. The boy on the beach in "Amor Fati" suggests that this child has a destiny associated with the aliens in some way and that Mulder plays a huge role in helping him to realize it.

After Scully safely gives birth and the true nature of William is determined, the alien replicants leave, probably returning to their regular human lives none the wiser. The game warden specifically says that this baby *must* be born. If like Krycek says they are truly afraid of what William is they would kill Scully immediately and destroy or take the child. They don't and Reyes–in her guise as a wise advisor knows that everything is going to be OK.

In fact, Billy and the other replicants are cast in the role of the shepherds from Luke's account of the birth of Christ or the astrologers from Matthew's. There is even a star in the sky or in actuality the Walk-Ins ' ship for them and Mulder to follow.

It is the super soldiers in Knowle Rohrer and Agent Crane with Krycek who really want the destruction or neutralization of William. They want total control and William represents the merging of man and the divine for *everyone* aliens and humans alike.

Originally in the narrative Krycek wanted the same thing Mulder does, but in the end as the shadow he sells out when he believes mankind is doomed or at least, his stake in the proceedings is. He is even willing to kill Mulder–albeit reluctantly–to cement the deal. Apparently Knowle Rohrer and Crane must promise him some kind of eternal life since he in turn, offers a thousand lives to Skinner if he shoots Mulder. Possibly Krycek is offered the chance to become a super soldier with its attending near immortality.

Skinner has no warm feelings for Krycek at all. He appears to be pretty unemotional about killing him and destroying the shadow. It's not surprising given that Krycek has been pulling his strings for a couple years with the nanobots. It's interesting to note that Krycek is not redeemed in the end of season eight; in fact, just the opposite–he makes the final step over to the dark side. However, there are myriad ways for the dead to rise on *The X-Files.*

In Krycek 's death scene, Mulder is basically presented with the same choice his father is– turn over his child to save the world–and he refuses to do so. In order to come full circle and restore those things that his father's decision destroys–family and love–he would have to choose the opposite–which he in fact does; this would be a fitting resolution for Mulder's journey.

By the end of the episode Doggett and Reyes have become partners on *The X-Files.* With all they have both seen in "Essence" and "Existence," including their investigation into Kersh's involvement, they should be sufficiently motivated to find their truth—whatever that may be. The x-files are now covered by a believer–who this time is subordinate to the skeptic–who gets feelings about stuff, and a skeptic whose disbelief isn't rooted in fact and hard science; a familiar dynamic, but with a different twist.

14

NOTHING IMPORTANT HAPPENED TODAY I

And so starts the season of Mulder's decent to the wounded king and the beginning of William's hero's journey. William is not his father though and like the hero Heracles has special abilities; he can move the mobile above his bed telekinetically.

Mulder leaves soon after William's birth and Scully refuses to divulge the reasons why to Doggett. She seems very nervous about the whole situation. Here Mulder makes the exact same mistake as Bill Mulder does. He abandons his child, the worst thing he could do as the hero in this myth.

The disinfecting water-supply additive, chloramine (made from chlorine and ammonia) may not be as innocuous as it appears. The super soldiers carry iron of some kind in their systems and are destroyed by coming into contact with magnetized iron ore. Iron is oxidized by chlorine, which changes it to the red color like that in the quarry in "Trust_No1." It is possible that the chloramine is intended to change the iron naturally occurring in the water supply into a form that is hazardous to the super soldiers. Shannon McMahon tells Doggett that she is trying to stop the super soldiers. She is killing the whistle-blowers on the chloramine project which makes sense if their activities threaten the chloramine project's intended agenda of destroying the existing super soldiers.

Shannon leaves Reyes and Doggett Wormus' obituary. She must have something to gain from their involvement. What does she want to see Scully about specifically? She obviously isn't there to take or harm William since she could easily get around Mrs. Scully if she wants to which reinforces that she's not acting on the super soldiers' behalf.

NOTHING IMPORTANT HAPPENED TODAY II

A ship that remains off-shore most of the time, houses a Project lab that appears to be manipulating ova for transplantation. The location of this lab is probably intended to make it less vulnerable to Billy Miles who is destroying this work.

Shannon tells Doggett, Reyes and Scully her story about becoming a super soldier and how much she hates it. Knowle Rohrer and she are supposedly the Adam and Eve of the super soldier program and are specifically chosen from Bravo Company in the Gulf; this just happens to be the same unit that Doggett was a member of. It appears more and more likely that Doggett is somehow either destined or set up to ultimately work on the x-files, or more likely to protect Scully and William.

Shannon McMahon tell Doggett, Reyes and Scully that she wants to stop the chloramine project when in reality her targets are the whistle-blowers and she appears to be protecting it instead. In any case, how would chloramine–even a mutated version of it–actually create super soldier offspring? Why would the super soldiers want to randomly create them to begin with; they want control and giving the general populace the same powers isn't working towards that end. It seems more likely that the chloramine program is intended to stop the super soldiers in some way and Shannon is lying about this aspect. She has to be lying about something.

Reyes speculates that McMahon is using them to find the third whistle-blower, which seems plausible. Reyes is frequently used as the voice of reason in the narrative. Perhaps to underscore her perceptiveness and ability to see (or feel) the real truth, Monica is definitely going to back Doggett up regardless of Folmer's supposed attempts to save her career; this is probably an intentional contrast against Mulder's behavior with *his* old flame Fowley. Monica isn't quite as blind to Folmer's duplicitous nature and doesn't fall for his manipulations as Mulder does Diana's.

Like Knowle Rohrer and the alien replicants Shannon has the metal vertebra. It would appear as though the Walk-Ins are fighting fire with fire. Shannon McMahon and Knowle Rohrer are working at cross-purposes. If nothing else, she wants Doggett alive–to the point of protecting him even after he's led her to the third whistle-blower, whereas Knowle obviously wants him dead. At no time does she spout the Mulder must die rhetoric. She does vaguely insinuate that William is a super soldier, but this may be to alert Scully to the potential dangers and to get her to begin investigating. She may have also hoped to get Scully to call Mulder home.

Scully does appear to be still concerned that William 's genetic origin is not purely human or normal and it isn't, although not for the reasons she suspects. She is still blind to the truth and is caught up in the lie.

Knowle Rohrer seems to be trying to find out more information on what's going on in the lab in an attempt to ascertain the Captain's intentions. He too is after the whistle-blowers and the Chloramine Project. He blows up the ship to protect the Project's work almost taking Scully, Reyes and Doggett with it.

Skinner is concerned about Scully's involvement with Doggett and his investigation thinking that it will endanger her and William. He wants her to tell Mulder about William's abilities and she refuses saying it will put Mulder in danger. Skinner tells her that they are *all* in danger. Mulder, like CSM is saving his own butt instead of protecting his family. Mulder's leaving doesn't make sense because it isn't supposed to.

Kersh insinuates that Scully is the one who asks Mulder to leave. However, based on the wording in Mulder's email in "Trust_No1" it would appear that Scully and Mulder came to their decision together. Both Mulder and Scully are acting against their normal MO and in order to understand the narrative purpose behind the separation it is very important to recognize that both of them make a serious mistake. These mistakes in judgment on both of their parts continue throughout the season. Since Scully is the one we get to see, it's very tempting to place all the blame on her shoulders. However, Mulder is just as culpable as she is and by having his actions play totally against his characterization the writers trying to point that out.

TRUSTNO1

> *"One day, you'll ask me to speak of a truth — of the miracle of your birth. To explain what is unexplained. And if I falter or fail on this day, know there is an answer, my child, a sacred imperishable truth, but one you may never hope to find alone. Chance meeting your perfect other, your perfect opposite — your protector and endangerer. Chance embarking with this other on the greatest of journeys — a search for truths fugitive and imponderable. If one day this chance may befall you, my son, do not fail or falter to seize it. The truths are out there. And if one day you should behold a miracle, as I have in you, you will learn the truth is not found in science, or on some unseen plane, but by looking into your own heart. And in that moment you will be blessed — and stricken. For the truest truths, are what hold us together, or keep us painfully, desperately apart."*

As they always are Scully's voice over is enlightening. Here is the idea of the perfect other or two halves of the balanced whole. It is also a comment on William's journey as the hero and where to find his truth–in his heart.

Scully tells Patti that she doesn't have anyone. It is a revealing comment, in that it underscores that Mulder's absence leaves her and William alone the one thing he should not have done. In the meantime, Doggett has become Mulder in a sense. He's after the truth as he sees it no matter what. Skinner points this out to him with no more success then he had previously with Mulder.

Based on Shadow Man's (a possible reference to the shadow archetype—this time the shadow of the Walk-Ins) comments and the surveillance photos from the opening montage it was obvious that Mulder and Scully had been under close surveillance for a very long time. Shadow Man is a super soldier and he makes it clear at the end that they do not want Mulder to have any influence on William. On the other hand the Walk-Ins do.

The super soldiers can be destroyed by something pertaining to the iron ore in the quarry. The analysis Doggett has done shows that their DNA can't be sequenced and that it has some connection to iron. In later episodes it's revealed that magnetite is their kryptonite, which suggests that the electro-magnetic force is responsible somehow.

PROVENANCE

Provenance: A place of origin.

"And you have to love him and raise him in spite of everything. Dana, god has given you a miracle. A child that wasn't supposed to be. Maybe it's not to question... just to be taken as a matter of faith."—Margaret Scully

The ship in Africa was millions of years old based on the fossil evidence found on its hull. This may suggest that the Walk-Ins are the origin of all life on this planet especially since traces of their DNA are still evident.

Now Scully believes that the ship in Africa was meant for her to find and not Mulder as she originally thought. This makes more sense in retrospect since it's likely that the ship or the shaman is directly responsible for restoring her fertility. Perhaps the Walk-Ins also need Scully to understand the significance of William and the nature of the divine and are hoping that she will eventually decipher the markings. If nothing else, it strongly implies that Scully was chosen to become William's mother and if that's so, then there must be a specific reason why. In any case, Scully has obviously has begun to realize that the aliens are somehow connected to mankind's notion of God.

The artifact reacts strongly to William's presence and does *not* attempt to hurt him. A similar artifact does something similar with a Bible in "Biogenesis" so it's likely that it is the artifact that moves closer to William on its own power and not William affecting the artifact. It is also revealed that the second ships symbols are different than the ship found in Africa. Perhaps the ships are arks of some kind–like the Ark of the Covenant in Judaic mythology. Here is the source or at the very least vessel of the power of the divine.

Agent Comer believes that William must die or something terrible will happen. He is neither an alien replicant nor a super soldier since he is not able to heal himself. A point is made of the fact that he is a straight shooter, which would imply that he thinks the right thing to do is to kill William now that he believes Mulder to be dead. Perhaps he understands that William's ultimate destiny as a creator or destroyer is directly connected to Mulder's influence. It appears that William will become a creator (as the boy is in "Amor Fati" with the ship) only if Mulder is in his life–underscoring yet again the terrible mistake Mulder and Scully make.

Skinner certainly seems to be waffling around again and keeps Scully, Doggett and Reyes in the dark. Since he's destroyed his shadow aspects when he kills Krycek, he must believe that he is protecting Scully by keeping information from her. This tactic never works in this narrative and it doesn't here.

Scully seems to be the most comfortable confiding in Reyes, which makes sense. Reyes is the most likely to believe her (although even she was having some difficulty buying into this one until the artifact did its thing) and she is the closest to Mulder in personality. Doggett is backing her up, but his motivations are different.

PROVIDENCE

Providence: God or nature's care or protection

"The bible says god appeared to Moses in a burning bush. He came to Jesus on a mountaintop. For Buddha, god came while he sat under a tree. God came to me in a vision in the desert, February 26, 1991. My recon squad had engaged Saddam's army in a small Bedouin encampment. We'd been ambushed, taken all by surprise and there were casualties. We were holding our perimeter, and we might've held up, but on this day I had a terrible sense of foreboding, I saw the future of those brave men, and they were about to die. Death came to take my men... but not me. I was left as a witness to a vision. Angels... from heaven. 'Behold, a whirlwind came out of the

north, and a brightness was about it. And out of the midst, came the likeness of four living creatures, and they had the likeness of a man." *[Ezekiel 1:4-5] "I knew why my life had been spared. That I was to deliver the message of these angels, of these sons of god, to deliver the message of the god who came before all other gods."*

Lieutenant Colonel Josepho voice over refers to the super soldiers, not to angels as he believes and sets up his mistake in perception and the resulting motivation.

The artifact can heal and since we've also seen the aliens (both in the form of the ABH and Jeremiah Smith in "Talitha Cumi," "Herrenvolk," and "This Is Not Happening") do the same thing, my guess is the underlying mechanism is the same. The artifact certainly seems to have some sort of sentience. It does, however, require direct contact with the skin since Comer wasn't healed of his burns until he takes it out of his pocket and he is not healed of the gun shot wounds at all.

The ships (at least the one from Africa and the one in Canada) have the word of God inscribed upon them and carry great power. There is also apparently a prophecy inscribed on it that tells of the birth of William and his role in leading the aliens as their savior.

The Walk-Ins as the divine will kill when it is necessary. They only do so to protect Mulder or William and to destroy the Project. Of all of the various agendas between the Consortium, the super soldiers, the Rebels, the Colonists and the Walk-Ins, *only* the Walk-Ins appear to want Mulder and William alive and together. The ship in Canada destroys Josepho and his followers when they try to force Scully to kill Mulder.

Reyes in her mythological role as the advisor gives Scully a big clue when she tells her that no religion would decree the death of an infant and that the information they receive comes from men (who are mistaken) and not from the divine. The information from the divine (Doggett's voice and the ships reaction and message in the markings) all point to a desire to protect William and Mulder's safety. The one thing that Scully truly does not understand and trust is in this protection.

WILLIAM

Oftentimes in myth a hero is taken or given away from his natural parents. Usually this is an attempt to forestall their destiny usually by a mother trying to protect her child. The important thing is that it *never* works; fate and the divine can not be circumvented. What actually happens is that the hero must face his destiny ignorant of his role and his choices reflect it. Think what could have happened if Mary had tried to protect Jesus from his fate. No matter how difficult it may be, a hero must walk his path and William is no different.

Mrs. Van Kamp just wants a healthy child with nothing wrong with it–something she is unlikely to get in the long run with William.

Jeffrey Spender returns badly disfigured from the injections that the Project doctors administer. He undergoes the same basic kind thing that the abductees and Mulder do (the chair even looks similar), with two important differences; it is done by humans not the

Walk-Ins and he is not healed in any way afterwards as Mulder is. In any case, whatever the doctors and scientists were trying to do fails left scarred for life.

Spender tells Scully; *"The conspiracy to keep the truth about aliens from the American public all but destroyed a few years ago, has given rise to a new conspiracy in the government now, by men who are alien themselves."* While everyone seems to think so, this is not a reference to the alien replicants, it's the super soldiers. They are basically alien but not of the aliens.

Spender injects William with magnetite–the super soldier kryptonite and they all believe William is now normal. The thing is, William isn't a super soldier and never was so this is unlikely to make much difference. If the aliens are the real threat to William and given the events in "Provenance"/"Providence" they aren't, then they will know where he is anyway no matter what Scully does. It's the same thing with the super soldiers who are the real threat. Based on "Trust_No1," it's obvious that they know what's going on at all times. Leaving William with an unsuspecting couple who only want a normal child probably isn't the smartest thing to do, but not for these reasons. The most important thing that everyone seems to know is that William 's destiny will be shaped by Mulder's influence or lack there of. Given that the Walk-Ins want it and the super soldiers don't it's a good bet that William 's future isn't going to go the way Scully hopes.

THE TRUTH

The most obvious way to view "The Truth" is as an episode that puts all of the pieces together and explains the mytharc. The problem with this is that a literal reading of the events of this episode as the real truth only serves to perpetuate a number of contradictions and requires the viewer to suspend a great deal of disbelief in the narrative. The other is as the final transformation of Mulder from the hero to the king–albeit a wounded and self-serving one just like his father Cigarette-Smoking Man. Let's see how each idea stacks up against the truth.

First and foremost is the idea that the aliens are an exclusively evil force out to destroy mankind either by enslaving it or using humans as biomaterial for reproducing themselves as seen in the movie and "The Beginning." This force is generally represented by the black oil or as alien bounty hunters, various clones or even sometimes as the little Grays. Even though they supposedly need mankind's help in creating a hybrid (either for an immune slave or as a host) sometime during the Gulf War they figured out a way to create super soldiers. By the end of the seventh season they have started to swap out key people with these replicants (here super soldiers and alien replicants are the same thing). For some reason they even use some members of Doggett's platoon for the first test subjects (Knowle Rohrer and Shannon McMahon). It's just a nice coincidence that Doggett is later partnered with Scully. Apparently the aliens want to use these super soldier bodies as their own and the immune hybrids as slaves (although the hybridization angle seems to have been dropped by the time the super soldiers start popping up). They feel that Mulder would be a good replication choice and abduct him. Good thing the Russians help them out and infect him with the black oil way back in the fourth season. Of course, according to Krycek in "Existence" they didn't even *know* that Scully is pregnant at the time of Mulder's abduction (and didn't find out until the events of "Per Manum" when Doggett inadvertently clues Rohrer in) so it ends up being a very convenient coincidence.

On the other hand, if the real point is that everyone is still ignorant of the real truth and are wrong about the aliens, then the obvious contradictions only underscore this. It is clear in

"Essence"/"Existence" that there are two groups; the alien replicants and the super soldiers with different agendas. No matter how similar they are physically, it is highly unlikely that they are one and the same. Instead like all the archetypes on the show, one (the super soldiers) is the shadow of the other (the alien replicants).

Next up is the chlorinated water. Since it's going to be pretty labor intensive (given what Mulder is subjected to) to abduct and turn everyone into replicants, the aliens also figured out a way to use chlorinated water and the chips to cause female abductees to suddenly become mysteriously pregnant with super soldier babies. Of course this apparently only works with a *select* few women, so just exactly how much labor–so to speak–they are ultimately hoping to save by 2012 is questionable.

The problem with this angle is that while Mary Hendershot from "Per Manum" does *not* require any male participation (presumably she was artificially inseminated without her knowledge) since the dates with her boyfriend didn't add up, Scully *does* require Mulder's genetic donation and William is *his* child too. Given that Scully is a doctor and scientist with genetic testing at her disposal, it's hard to believe that she wouldn't do a paternity test just to make sure given everything she's been told. Again, while the narrative ostensibly puts forth the aliens as the bad guys, the real truth is revealed in the actual events, not the characters' interpretations of them.

The IVF fails–either no embryo is created because the ova are unviable (IVF is done *outside* of the mother 's body) and there is no implantation to begin with or the embryos don't take after they are implanted and no hormonal change occurs and they are absorbed by Scully's body. Regardless it's impossible for Scully to have gotten pregnant this way–unless an embryo just hung around for awhile (maybe it hid behind her bladder or something) without affecting Scully's physiology until it decides to become a pregnancy at a later date; pretty big trick even for a super soldier.

The third point is that the powers that be are apparently in on the whole thing and have negotiated a deal where they are going to be allowed by the aliens to hide out at Mount Weather after colonization begins. It must be humanity that the shadow (there's that archetype) government is planning on hiding from since the super soldiers and in this telling the aliens since they are one and the same, know all about the secret base at Mount Weather. Knowle Rohrer is hanging out there after all. What exactly does the shadow government have left to deal with anyway?

Instead it is more likely that the members of the shadow government along with their super soldiers are hoping that they can hide from the aliens. They are still operating under a misconception of what colonization will be and believe it to be an invasion. It's nothing of the sort, but that's the *truth* that everyone (including Mulder) seems unable to see.

The fourth point is that these same powers that be also *know* that magnetite is the aliens' form of kryptonite but they are apparently not smart enough to figure out how to use that knowledge to build some kind of weapon. They *do*, however, have some kind of serum that will neutralize one–at least when it's a baby since Spender uses it on William in the mistaken belief that he is a super soldier.

This begs the question, if there is no symbiosis or duality what is William *after* he's injected? If the alien sentience is destroyed then what's left? Does he have a human sentience too that has been suppressed since he is born or is his special powers the only thing that is neutralized and he is still in effect an alien as far as his mind goes? He sure seems like a pretty sweet little guy for an evil alien in disguise.

The fifth point is that the aliens aren't exactly geniuses either, given that all it takes to hide William from them is to put him through the adoption system. You'd think that a group capable of constant surveillance and sneaky swap outs of key folks would be able to get to any sealed records and the Van Kamps would be toast. Then again, these are apparently the same aliens that leave William with Scully right after he is born and let Mulder live (even though they also appear to want him dead) when they have the *perfect* opportunity to take care of things once and for all when both are completely vulnerable in Georgia with a whole bunch of the replicants around. Apparently the aliens have short attention spans and are easily distracted from their goals since they never seem to finish what they appear to start. Then again, there must be *some* reason they want William to stay with Scully since the ship in "Providence" torches a group of people who are working *for* their cause just so they can return William to her. Maybe they just don't want to deal with poopy diapers.

Or it could be that the aliens do want Scully and Mulder to be William's parents and what they have actually been doing is trying to ensure that, but Mulder and Scully try to second-guess them and do the absolutely worse thing they can. The Walk-Ins may try to show the heroes the way, but they will *not* make their choices for them. That's something the Consortium and the super soldiers never do.

The sixth point is that Mulder apparently doesn't want to deal with poopy diapers either and he cuts and runs as soon as he has a half-way plausible reason to do so–a warning about *his* life being in danger from Kersh, someone who has *never* told them the truth (another fine example of Mulder's version of "trust no one"). Of course antsy Mulder must have gotten bored while he's off supposedly keeping his heroic butt safe (at the expense of Scully and William 's) since he decides to believe a note from an anonymous wise man and puts himself in direct danger at Mount Weather (there he goes with the trust thing again). He does finally find his version of the all-important truth which turns out to be the date of colonization. The fact that this is something he could have figured out as early as "Red Museum" if he had just paid attention isn't really mentioned.

Of course, he decides that he can't tell anyone what he's found. When the Consortium does this it's a great evil, when Mulder does it, it's a self-sacrificing heroic gesture. Then again, his whole quest is righteous and heroic just *because* he won't give up, regardless of how much pain and death it causes without actually *producing* anything positive. Never mind that the villain CSM acts exactly the same way and is demonized for it. Even though this date is more important than he and Scully, he's prepared to die without telling anyone about it, in other words in vain. In any case, the so-called trial isn't going to do anything positive for his quest given that it is being held completely in secret and it's result is a foregone conclusion. In fact, it isn't clear what exactly Mulder thinks he *is* going to accomplish besides a form of suicide.

Or this could be intended to be a very strong indication that Mulder has *failed* to transform and is now becoming the destructive wounded king.

The seventh point is that later Cigarette-Smoking Man has finally decided to tell the truth and tells Mulder that the Mayan were so afraid of the colonization date that their calendar stops there. Of course Cigarette-Smoking Man is still up to his old tricks and that's not really how the Mayan's viewed this date at all, they saw it as the beginning of an enlightened age, exactly how the Walk-Ins characterize it in "Red Museum."

The ninth point is that Scully is able to overlook all of the things she's lost (most especially the child she was desperate to have) due to Mulder's obsessive–oops, heroic–quest and would do it all again, just because he *won't give up*! In other words, the end justifies the means (as long as you're the good guy) even if that end doesn't amount to much. Again, this is exactly the Consortium 's policy. As long as one's myopic view is never relinquished regardless of the evidence, one is a hero worth following no matter how much damage it may cause others. Here is instead yet another illustration of Mulder becoming that which he despised.

Scully may finally have come to believe in aliens, but at what cost? In doing so she seems to have lost her ability to think logically and her faith in science–the two things that according to Mulder in the movie save him a hundred times over.

According to the surface "truth" in this episode by the end of it Mulder has come to believe in a force more powerful than the aliens and which is presumably the Christian notion of God as represented by Scully's cross. He believes that this force speaks through the dead and will tell he and Scully how to save *themselves* (again the save your own butt rhetoric of the Consortium). Even so, Mulder decides to completely *ignore* what the dead–the Lone Gunmen at least–are actually telling him to do so it's unclear how committed he actually is to the idea. Again this is more appropriate in illustrating the failure of the hero than it is in his successful transformation.

Throughout the show Mulder has been led around by his nose by Cigarette-Smoking Man or by a more intimate part of his body if it's Diana who is doing the leading. He's still falling for it in "The Truth." Perhaps it's supposed to be uplifting as long as one makes the requisite heroic speech while doing it. The show's staple "Trust No One" mantra doesn't even win in the end, Mulder still trusts anyone who tells him what he wants to hear and ignores those who don't, even dead friends who inexplicitly show up and tell him to get over his messiah complex. But hey, he's the hero so whatever he believes *has* to be the truth–even if it comes from the bad guy. Then again, maybe not and that is the *real* point, because the contradictions only disappear if you stop buying that Mulder and Scully have a clue about what's really going on and if you're able to accept that sometimes the good guys may *not* know the best course of action and that real heroism may lie in knowing when to *change* one's point of view instead of holding fast to it no matter how much harm it causes or how much actual evidence (versus hearsay) there is against it. Maybe Mulder's right in the end after all–he's a guilty man.

15

THE CONCLUSION

One of the big differences between fairy tale and myth is that in myth the hero often fails, generally because they try to thwart fate or refuse to accept the divine boon. As mythic hero, Mulder is no exception and he too ultimately fails, although he does achieve self-enlightenment through that failure just as most failed heroes generally do. Today's popular heroes tend to always win and are always righteous in their beliefs, which may make it very difficult to accept the more classic idea of the hero 's failure. *The X-Files'* mythology, however, follows the classic form, not the popular one.

Humans fail all the time and even periodically succeed; we pick ourselves up and try again. However, Mulder and Scully do this *over* and *over* again throughout the life of the show– that's the trial stage. The mythic hero 's journey is cyclical; it begins and goes through stages where the hero is moved forward in some way. In the end, the hero must face a choice, live the truth he's found or reject it. In *The X-Files* particular type of hero 's journey–the hero generally becomes the next king personified here by Cigarette-Smoking Man, but how the hero as the new king will rule is based on the choice he makes and the world is either healed or damaged by the nature of the hero's stewardship of the divine boon. Does the hero learn the valuable lesson the divine is trying to teach him or does he choose to ignore it–as both CSM and Mulder do?

On *The X-Files* William is the boon, the gift from the divine that the hero can bring back to transform the world or choose to reject and return to his old ways. In order for the boon to work, the hero *has* to respect and take care of it– just as the Grail King is supposed to become the steward of the grail–not toss it aside when it becomes inconvenient or troublesome. Unfortunately this is basically what Mulder and Scully do from a mythic perspective. It's akin to Parsifal finding the Grail and then saying that he'd rather continue searching for it in some other form that's more to his liking than take his rightful place as the next Grail King. The Grail 's ability to heal the land or render it a wasteland is *directly* tied to the Grail King's worthiness to protect it. Perhaps this is the point that Chris Carter is trying to make with the whole William will become either a tool for good or evil based on Mulder's influence angle.

Another illustration of the notion of stewardship of the boon is the epic Sumerian myth of Gilgamesh. Gilgamesh wants immortality (his hero cycle is *very* self-centered, the world at stake is his own, not the larger one) and he finds it in the form of a plant from the divine world. However, he fails in his steward-ship of the plant and it is carried off by a snake and Gilgamesh fails to achieve immortality (or his transformation), however, he *does* gain valuable insight. But that insight doesn't restore the boon to him, it's just a lesson that he's now learned that will hopefully affect how he lives out the rest of his life.

Mulder completes his mythic journey in "Existence" and his decision to leave in "Nothing Important Happened Today" is a rejection of the truth he finds and the result is the restart of the hero 's cycle with him now in CSM's shadow king archetypal role and William as the next hero who must either heal or destroy him. The events of the ninth season are an illustration of the conse-quences of rejecting the boon. Scully's later decision to put William up for adoption isn't analogous to Bill Mulder's decision with Samantha; instead Mulder's decision to leave his family in order to follow his quest is the same basic idea and the same choice. Both Bill and Mulder break up the family while in single-minded pursuit of something else—for Bill it is the vaccine, for Mulder it's *his* version of the truth. There is an even closer analogy with Mulder/Ciga-rette-Smoking Man—CSM abandons Cassandra and Jeffrey to continue his quest for heroic glorification and Mulder basically does the exact same thing. He is still fixated on the idea that *he* alone can alter the course of destiny through direct intervention instead of accepting that his real place is as the father of the messianic child. Mulder wants to sacrifice himself and be Christ instead of becoming Joseph, which would require him to come down from the cross of his own making and live his life.

Throughout the show there is an underlying theme of father's influencing their sons, whether that's Bill Mulder influencing Mulder to chase the monsters out of his own guilt over what happens to Samantha, or CSM creating Mulder to support his own agenda. Since William's destiny is changes—through Jeffrey Spender's nullification of his power—by leaving Mulder *does* influence his son, just not in the way the divine intends him to. Mulder's choice to flee to the desert *without* Scully and William is where he goes astray of the right path and is what ultimately leaves William vulnerable to Spender in the first place.

By the time the series finale "The Truth" rolls around it's too late for Mulder to suddenly see the light, he already made the fateful choice to leave and reject the boon in "Nothing Important Happened Today I" and the damage is done. That doesn't mean that things are hopeless though, it means that the cycle has to start again, this time with William as the new hero searching for the divine truth and Mulder as the fading king that must be redeemed or destroyed. William as Grail/boon and Mulder as hero is moot at this point. William's adoption is an illustration that he has now become the next hero instead–this is a *very* typical beginning for a hero–and Mulder's final scene with CSM is an illustration that he has become the Fisher King like his father before him.

Does Mulder learn something important in the end–sure, or at least I hope he does–but does that knowledge *fix* the damage his choice already caused? It shouldn't from a mythological perspective. Mulder's final transformation in "The Truth" may affect how he later interacts with William as king and hero, and *that* may be the thing that allows *William* to ultimately make the right choice in regards to the boon when it's his time to do so; which in turn may finally heal the world.

The importance of free will is illustrated in the ninth season episode "Improbable," the divine in *The X-Files* universe will only attempt to guide, not actively change the decision of the killer to kill. The same idea of free will in the mytharc requires that the Walk-Ins let Mulder's actions stand regardless of the consequences; otherwise free will has no real meaning. Their influence is to allow another chance with a *new* hero in a new cycle–although given the Dec. 12, 2012 deadline, time is quickly running out. Can William correct his father's mistakes or is it over and the ultimate fate of the world decided?

finis

BIBLIOGRAPHY

Al-Khalili, Jim, 2003, *Quantum, A Guide for the Perplexed*, London, Weidenfeld & Nicolson

Alper, Matthew, 2001, The "God" Part of the Brain, New York, Rogue Press

Baring, Anne & Cashford, Jules, 1991, *The Myth of the Goddess - Evolution of an Image*, London, Penguin Books

Bettelheim, Bruno, 1975, *The Uses of Enchantment - The Meaning and Importance of Fairy Tales*, New York, Random House

Bierlein, J.F., 1994, *Parallel Myths*, New York, Ballantine Wellspring Book

Bulfinch, Thomas, 1959, Bulfinch's Mythology, New York, Doubleday

Callahan, Tim, 2002, *Secret Origins of the Bible*, Altadena, Millennium Press

Campbell, Joseph, 1970, *Myths, Dreams, and Religion*, New York, MJF Books

Campbell, Joseph, 1949, *The Hero with a Thousand Faces*, New York, Princeton-Bollingen

Campbell, Joseph with Bill Moyers, 1988, *The Power of Myth*, New York, Doubleday

Campbell, Joseph, 1990, *Transformations of Myth Through Time*, New York, Harper & Row Publishers

Clancy, Susan A., 2005, *Abducted - How People Come to Believe They Were Kidnapped by Aliens*, Cambridge, Harvard University Press

Colum, Padriaic, 1996, *Nordic Gods and Heroes*, New York, Dover Publications

Dixon-Kennedy, Mike, 1995, *Arthurian Myth & Legend - An A-Z of People and Places*, Great Britain, Brockhampton Press

Edinger, Edward F., 1972, *Ego and Archetype*, Boston, Shambhala Publications

Erdoes, Richard & Oritz, Alfonso, 1984, *American Indian Myths and Legends*, New York, Pantheon Books

Evola, Julius, 1994, *The Mystery of the Grail - Initiation and Magic in the Quest for Spirit*, Rochester, Inner Traditions

Greene, Liz & Sharman-Burke, Juliet, 2000, *The Mythic Journey - The Meaning of Myth as a Guide for Life*, New York, Simon & Schuster

Gribbin, John, 1984, *In Search of Schrodinger's Cat*, New York, Bantam Books

Gribbin, John, 1995, *Schrodinger's Kittens and the Search for Reality*, New York, Little, Brown & Company

Hamer, Dean, 2004, How Faith is Hardwired into Our Genes, New York, Doubleday

Hamilton, Edith, 1942, *Mythology*, New York, Warner Books

Jung, C.G., 1982, *Aspects of the Feminine*, Princeton, Princeton University Press

Jung, C.G., 1989, *Aspects of the Masculine*, Princeton, Princeton University Press

Jung, C.G., 1959, *Four Archetypes*, Princeton, Princeton University Press

Jung, C.G., 1964, *Man and His Symbols*, New York, Doubleday

Jung, Emma & von Franz, Marie-Lousie, 1960, *The Grail Legend*, Princeton, Princeton University Press

Kaltreider, Kurt Ph.D., 2004, *American Indian Cultural Heroes and Teaching Tales*, Carlsbad, Hay House Inc.

Kelly, Lynne, 2004, *The Skeptic's Guide to the Paranormal*, New York, Thunder's Mouth Press

Leeming, David & Page, Jake, 1998, *The Mythology of Native North America*, Norman, University of Oklahoma Press

Loftus, Dr. Elizabeth, 1994, *The Myth of Repressed Memory*, New York, St. Martin's Press

Marshall, Ian & Zohar, Danah, 1997, *Who's Afraid of Schrodinger's Cat?*, New York, Quill William Morrow

Mercantante, Anthony S., 1978, *Good and Evil in Myth & Legend*, New York, Barnes & Noble Books

Meyer, Rudolf, 1981, *The Wisdom of Fairy Tales*, Great Britain, Florris Books

Nicholson, Shirley, 1987, *Shamanism*, Wheaton, Quest Books

Rosenberg, Donna, 1994, World Mythology, 3rd Edition, Chicago, NTC Publishing Group

Sagan, Carl, 1996, *The Demon-Haunted World*, New York, Ballantine Books

Sexton, James D., 1992, *Mayan Folktales - Folklore from Lake Atitlan, Guatemala*, Albuquerque, University of New Mexico Press

Stevens, Anthony, 1998, *Ariadne's Clue - A Guide to the Symbols of Humankind*, Princeton, Princeton University Press

Tedlock, Dennis, 1985, *Popol Vuh - The Definitive Edition of the Mayan Book of the Dawn of Life and the Glories of Gods and Kings*, New York, Simon & Schuster

Vogler, Christopher, 1998, *The Writer's Journey, Mythic Structure for Writers*, Studio City, Michael Wiese Productions

von Franz, Marie-Louise, 1995, *Shadow and Evil in Fairy Tales*, Boston, Shambhala

Printed in Great Britain
by Amazon